CHINESE COOKING

CHINESE COOKING

Distributed in the U.S.A.
by Galahad Books
a division of
A&W Promotional Corporation
95 Madison Avenue, New York,
N.Y. 10016

©1975 Cathay Books

ISBN 0 904644 04 9

Produced by
Madarin Publishers Ltd.,
Hong Kong.

Printed in Hong Kong

CONTENTS

Serving a Chinese meal

INTRODUCTION

Chinese food is becoming increasingly popular in the West as the existence of numerous Chinese restaurants testifies. But most people still hesitate to cook it at home in the belief that there is a mystery about Chinese cooking which the Western mind cannot fathom. In reality, it is remarkably simple, economic and practical. As there are no rigid rules or precise quantities, there is also plenty of scope for imagination and inventiveness. Far from being a chore, Chinese cooking is a creative activity and the blending of colours, tastes and textures can give a great deal of aesthetic satisfaction as well as satisfying the appetite.

PREPARATION AND COOKING

As Chinese food is eaten with chopsticks, it is usually cut into very small pieces – thinly sliced, shredded or diced. If a whole joint of meat or a duck or chicken is being served, it is usually cooked very slowly until tender enough to be pulled apart with chopsticks.

Stir-frying is the most commonly used method of cooking. For this, the food is cut into small pieces and fried very quickly in just a little oil or fat. It is the combination of speed and fierce heat which produces the crispness characteristic of Chinese cooking. The meat, fish or poultry is usually fried first, then removed from the pan while accompanying vegetables are cooked and returned to the pan with seasoning and often a little liquid in the form of sherry, soy sauce or stock.

The actual cooking is often performed in less than 5 minutes; with this method it is the preparation of ingredients which takes the time. But with forethought and good organization, much of it can be done in advance: stock can be made; meat can be marinated; dried food can be soaked, and hard vegetables can be shredded and kept in the refrigerator for a short time. Leftover food may also be used in stir-fried dishes.

Other methods – stewing, braising and steaming – involve longer cooking but less preparation. Care should be taken with the choice of ingredients to be steamed as this method of cooking is a test of the quality of the food. When braising and stewing, however, cheaper cuts may be used as the long, slow cooking renders even the toughest meat tender.

UTENSILS

In China the most commonly used cooking utensil is the wok, a large rounded pan which is used for frying, boiling and simmering. But ordinary saucepans and frying pans serve the purpose equally well. It is an advantage to have a frying pan with a lid as many recipes require the food to be covered for a short time while cooking.

A steamer is a useful item, but if you do not own one, use a dish standing in a saucepan containing a few inches of simmering water. A heavy enamelled casserole dish is ideal for long slow cooking on the stove or in the oven. Two indispensable utensils are a sharp kitchen knife (or chopper, if you have one) and a chopping board, because there is a great deal of chopping, slicing and shredding involved in the preparation of Chinese food.

The Chinese use chopsticks for most cooking operations but, unless you are skilled in their manipulation, it is easier to use a wooden spoon, perforated spoon, tongs or fish slice as appropriate. As the flavour of Chinese food is very delicate it can be easily tainted with metal, so try to use wooden spoons and china or glass bowls where possible.

INGREDIENTS

The basic ingredients are the same as those used in the West and many of the flavourings, such as garlic, sherry, chilli and spring onions (scallions), are commonly used in Western kitchens; others, like soy sauce, monosodium glutamate and fresh ginger, are available in good supermarkets and, of course, Chinese stores. Basic ingredients are dealt with in the relevant chapters; listed below are the flavourings and special Chinese foods you will need for recipes in this book.

Almonds, browned (toasted)
Brown (toast) the almonds by placing in the grill pan and heating under a hot grill, stirring occasionally, until golden.

Bamboo shoots
Available already cooked and ready to use from Chinese stores (raw roots need to be boiled for a long time), or in cans from some supermarkets. Some cans have the shoots already sliced.

Bean sprouts
Fresh bean sprouts can be bought from Chinese food stores; canned ones are available in supermarkets, but these should be rinsed and drained before use.

Black beans (Chinese dried)
Available canned from larger supermarkets.

Ginger
Fresh, or green, ginger is the root of the ginger plant and can be bought at Chinese grocers or Indian stores and some supermarkets. Powdered, or ground, ginger is rarely used as a substitute.

Hoi sin sauce
Available canned from Chinese food stores.

Lychees
These can sometimes be bought fresh from good greengrocers and even some street markets.

Monosodium glutamate
This a flavouring or taste powder which is sold under different names throughout the world: Ve-tsin; Ac'cent in Britain and the USA; taste or gourmet powder; Zip in Australia.

Mushrooms
Chinese dried mushrooms are available from Chinese food stores. They have a distinctive flavour so fresh mushrooms would not give the same results, nor would the continental dried mushrooms.

Oyster sauce
Available canned from Chinese food stores.

Sesame oil
This is used as a flavouring, not for frying.

Sesame seeds
Available from health food stores.

Snow peas (mange-tout)
Available from greengrocers and Chinese food stores when in season.

Soy sauce
This is probably the most widely used flavouring in Chinese cooking. It is widely available and can be used in a large variety of dishes. It is always used in red-cooked dishes, which take their name from the reddish-brown colour created by the sauce in cooking. There is a substitute called Vesop which is also widely available; some people consider it to be better than soy sauce for soups and vegetables dishes.

Star anise
Available from Chinese food stores.

Water chestnuts
A crisp Chinese vegetable; available from Chinese food stores and some supermarkets.

PLANNING A MEAL

A Chinese meal is a communal one and as such it provides a delightfully informal way of entertaining as the dishes are placed on the table and diners help themselves to a little from each dish. For four people, serve three to four main dishes plus soup and rice, followed by a dessert if wished; accompaniments such as crispy noodles and spring rolls may also be served. For each additional person, add one dish. In choosing a menu, select dishes which give a good balance of colour, texture and flavour.

When cooking several dishes, it is advisable to have at least one slowly cooked dish so that it can be left to cook at the back of the stove or in the oven while you prepare the other dishes. Have the rice and soup cooking on the back of the stove while you prepare stir-fried dishes on the front burners. In this way, and with many of the ingredients prepared beforehand, it is possible to produce a meal of 4–6 dishes with perfect timing and with the minimum of fuss.

If wine is required with the meal, choose a light, dry white wine and serve China tea at the end of the meal. Some people like to drink China tea throughout the meal.

A selection of Chinese ingredients

WEIGHTS AND MEASURES

Abbreviations

oz.	ounce	kg.	kilogramme
lb.	pound	dcl.	decilitre (1/10 litre)
g.	gramme	l.	litre

Metric and American equivalents
Approximate metric equivalents have been given: they have been scaled up or down slightly to make weighing and measuring easier. Where a slight difference may alter the consistency, as in the case of doughs or biscuits, more precise equivalents have been given. American equivalents are given in a separate column.

Can sizes
As can sizes vary, the approximate weight has been given: simply buy the can nearest to this weight.

SUGGESTED MENUS FOR FOUR PEOPLE

Raindrop soup
Sweet and sour prawns (shrimp)
Chicken dice with fried walnuts
Pork and bamboo shoots
Fried lettuce
Boiled or steamed rice
Gingered fruit

Tomato soup with egg flower
Shellfish fritters
Braised chicken with peppers
Stewed lamb with orange
Fried celery cabbage
Fried rice
Almond cream with chow chow

Watermelon soup
Pineapple fish
Duck with almonds
Spiced whole lamb
Broccoli with pork
Boiled or steamed rice
Almond biscuits

Mixed vegetable soup
Scallops with peppers
Crisp skin chicken
Pork with mushrooms
Fried spinach
Boiled or steamed rice
Almond lake with mandarin oranges

MEAT

To the Chinese meat usually means pork, for this is the most commonly used meat in Chinese cooking. Beef and lamb are also eaten, but to a lesser extent, and goat meat is eaten in the hilly region of the south. Most of the recipes in this chapter are, therefore, for pork.

As the meat is usually cut into small pieces and cooked quickly, it is important to use good quality lean meat such as pork fillet and tenderloin, steaks, rump, sirloin and topside, shoulder and leg of lamb. Although this may seem extravagant, it is relatively economical because the quantities are usually quite small, as they are used in conjunction with other ingredients.

The preparation of the meat is also important. Slices should be paper-thin and about 1 inch (2·5 cm.) square; shreds of meat should be no wider than they are thin and cubes should be $\frac{1}{2}$–1 inch (1·25–2·5 cm.) square. A little practice is required to achieve these results, but it helps to use a sharp kitchen knife and to cut across the grain of the meat. Meat balls are better made with slightly fattier meat as the fat prevents them being too dry; they are usually small, from the size of a golf ball to a walnut.

When poultry and meat are cooked whole and in joints, they are usually stewed or braised until they can be picked to pieces with chopsticks.

PORK AND EGGS

IMPERIAL/METRIC	AMERICAN	METHOD
2 lb./1 kg. lean pork	2 lb. lean pork	Cut the meat into 1 inch dice, put into a pan with the water, bring to the boil, remove the scum, cover and simmer for 30 minutes. Add the soy sauce, sherry and salt. Cook for another 30 minutes.
1 pint/½ litre water	2½ cups water	
4 tablespoons soy sauce	⅓ cup soy sauce	
2 tablespoons sherry	2 tablespoons sherry	
1 teaspoon salt	1 teaspoon salt	Boil the eggs for 8 minutes, cool and remove the shells. Make a small slit in the side of each egg and add to the pork. Chop the spring onions (scallions), add to the pan and simmer very gently for 5 minutes.
6 eggs	6 eggs	
6 spring onions	6 scallions	

BARBECUED PORK WITH BEAN SPROUTS

IMPERIAL/METRIC	AMERICAN	METHOD
1 lb./½ kg. lean pork	1 lb. lean pork	Cut pork into strips 2 inches by 1 inch by 1 inch. Chop spring onion (scallion) finely; mix with the ginger, soy sauce, sherry and garlic in an oblong dish. Add the pork strips, coat with the marinade and leave for 4–6 hours, stirring occasionally.
1 spring onion	1 scallion	
2 × ¼ inch slices fresh ginger	2 × ¼ inch slices fresh ginger	
4 tablespoons hoi sin or soy sauce	⅓ cup hoi sin or soy sauce	
2 tablespoons dry sherry	2 tablespoons dry sherry	Drain the pork and rub it with honey. Place on a greased rack in a roasting pan containing 1 inch of water. Cook for 25 minutes at 350°F/180°C, Mark 4. Slice into thin pieces.
1 clove garlic, crushed	1 clove garlic, crushed	
2 tablespoons honey	2 tablespoons honey	
1 tablespoon peanut oil	1 tablespoon peanut oil	
1 teaspoon very finely chopped fresh ginger	1 teaspoon very finely chopped fresh ginger	Heat the oil in a saucepan, add the chopped ginger and salt and fry for 2 minutes. Drain the bean sprouts, rinse in cold running water, drain again and add to the saucepan with 1 tablespoon of water and the sugar. Heat gently, stirring until well mixed. Add the pork, cover, and heat through.
½ teaspoon salt	½ teaspoon salt	
1 lb./½ kg. bean sprouts	1 lb. bean sprouts	
1 teaspoon sugar	1 teaspoon sugar	

PORK AND MUSHROOM BALLS WITH VEGETABLES

IMPERIAL/METRIC	AMERICAN	METHOD
4 dried mushrooms	4 dried mushrooms	Soak mushrooms in warm water for 20 minutes, rinse, squeeze dry and chop finely; discard the stalks. Mix thoroughly the pork, mushrooms, a little cornflour (cornstarch), sherry, salt and pepper. Form mixture into balls and roll them in cornflour (cornstarch).
¾ lb./375 g. minced pork	¾ lb. ground pork	
cornflour	cornstarch	
½ tablespoon dry sherry	½ tablespoon dry sherry	
salt and pepper	salt and pepper	
1 onion, sliced	1 onion, sliced	Cut the celery diagonally. Skin, deseed and slice the tomatoes. Drain bean sprouts, rinse in running water and drain again. Heat the oil in a saucepan and fry the pork and mushroom balls until golden. Cover and cook very gently for a further 6–8 minutes. Remove and add the onion, celery, tomatoes and water chestnuts. Fry, stirring, for 5 minutes.
2 sticks celery	2 sticks celery	
4 tomatoes	4 tomatoes	
6 water chestnuts, sliced	6 water chestnuts, sliced	
½ lb./250 g. bean sprouts	½ lb. bean sprouts	
2 tablespoons peanut oil	2 tablespoons peanut oil	
¼ pint/1 dcl. chicken stock	¾ cup chicken stock	Pour off any oil and add the chicken stock blended with 1 tablespoon cornflour (cornstarch), salt and soy sauce. Bring to the boil, stirring, and simmer for 2–3 minutes. Add the bean sprouts and pork and mushroom balls and reheat.
1 tablespoon soy sauce	1 tablespoon soy sauce	

Pork and eggs

*Pork balls with cabbage
and Pork with sweet and pungent sauce*

PORK BALLS WITH CABBAGE

IMPERIAL/METRIC	AMERICAN
1 lb./½ kg. lean pork	1 lb. lean pork
2 tablespoons soy sauce	2 tablespoons soy sauce
1 tablespoon sherry	1 tablespoon sherry
2 teaspoons salt	2 teaspoons salt
1 tablespoon cornflour	1 tablespoon cornstarch
1 lb./½ kg. cabbage	1 lb. cabbage
3 spring onions	3 scallions
oil for frying	oil for frying

METHOD

Mince (grind) the meat and add half the soy sauce, all the sherry, half the salt and all the cornflour (cornstarch). Beat well until evenly blended. Shape the mixture into 12 balls.

Cut the cabbage into 2 inch pieces and chop the spring onions (scallions); heat the oil and fry the vegetables for 2–3 minutes, stirring constantly. Add ½ pint (¼ litre/1¼ cups) water, the remaining soy sauce and salt; bring to the boil. Place the meat balls on top, cover and cook for 15 minutes.

PORK WITH SWEET AND PUNGENT SAUCE

IMPERIAL/METRIC	AMERICAN
1 lb./½ kg. shoulder of pork	1 lb. shoulder of pork
4 tablespoons soy sauce	⅓ cup soy sauce
2 cloves star anise	2 cloves star anise
3 tablespoons brown sugar	3 tablespoons brown sugar
¾ pint/3½ dcl. chicken stock	2 cups chicken stock
1 carrot	1 carrot
1 small red or green pepper	1 small red or green pepper
4 pineapple rings	4 pineapple rings
¼ pint/1 dcl. water	½ cup water
2 tablespoons vinegar	2 tablespoons vinegar
1 teaspoon very finely chopped fresh ginger	1 teaspoon very finely chopped fresh ginger
1 clove garlic, crushed	1 clove garlic, crushed
1 tablespoon tomato paste	1 tablespoon tomato paste
½ teaspoon salt	½ teaspoon salt
1 tablespoon dry sherry	1 tablespoon dry sherry
1 tablespoon cornflour	1 tablespoon cornstarch

METHOD

Cut pork into long thin strips. Mix marinade of soy sauce, star anise, 1 tablespoon brown sugar and the chicken stock. Marinate the pork for about 2 hours. Place the pork and marinade in a saucepan, bring to the boil, stirring, simmer for 20 minutes and drain.

Cut the carrot and pepper into wedges, drop into a pan of boiling water and simmer for 5 minutes. Drain. Cut pineapple rings into eighths. Place all the ingredients in a saucepan; bring to the boil, stirring constantly, and simmer for 3–4 minutes.

PORK AND CARROTS

IMPERIAL/METRIC	AMERICAN
2 lb./1 kg. pork spareribs	2 lb. pork spareribs
1 pint/½ litre water	2½ cups water
4 tablespoons soy sauce	⅓ cup soy sauce
2 tablespoons sherry	2 tablespoons sherry
1 teaspoon salt	1 teaspoon salt
1 teaspoon ground ginger	1 teaspoon ground ginger
1 lb./½ kg. young carrots	1 lb. young carrots

METHOD

Wipe and cut the spareribs into individual ribs. Put them into a large pan with the water, bring to the boil, remove the scum, and cover the pan with a tight fitting lid. Simmer for 1 hour. Add the soy sauce, sherry, salt and ginger. Mix well. Scrub the carrots and cut into 1 inch lengths. Add to the pan and cook for a further 30 minutes.

PORK AND PEANUTS

IMPERIAL/METRIC	AMERICAN
½ lb./250 g. uncooked peanuts	½ lb. uncooked peanuts
1 teaspoon salt	1 teaspoon salt
1 teaspoon oil	1 teaspoon oil
1 lb./½ kg. lean pork	1 lb. lean pork
1 teaspoon cornflour	1 teaspoon cornstarch
1 tablespoon soy sauce	1 tablespoon soy sauce
1 tablespoon sherry	1 tablespoon sherry
1 clove garlic	1 clove garlic
2 tablespoons oil	2 tablespoons oil
4 oz./125 g. fresh mushrooms	4 oz. fresh mushrooms
2 sticks celery	2 sticks celery
2 spring onions	2 scallions
1 tablespoon oyster sauce	1 tablespoon oyster sauce
¼ pint/1 dcl. stock or water	¾ cup stock or water

METHOD

Shell the nuts, sprinkle with salt and fry in the oil for 2–3 minutes. Drain on kitchen paper. Cut the pork into shreds, add the cornflour (cornstarch), soy sauce and sherry. Crush the garlic, add to the meat and mix well. Heat the oil in another pan and fry the meat quickly, stirring all the time, for 2 minutes.

Wash and slice the mushrooms; wash and thinly slice the celery; chop the spring onions (scallions). Add the vegetables to the pan with the oyster sauce, nuts and stock or water. Cook for 3 minutes.

WHOLE PORK SHOULDER

IMPERIAL/METRIC	AMERICAN
5 lb./2½ kg. shoulder of pork	5 lb. shoulder of pork
6 tablespoons soy sauce	½ cup soy sauce
6 tablespoons sherry	½ cup sherry
1 tablespoon brown sugar	1 tablespoon brown sugar
4 spring onions	4 scallions
1 oz./30 g. fresh ginger	1 oz. fresh ginger

METHOD

Put the meat in a large bowl of cold water to soak overnight. Drain. Put the pork in a large pan with enough water to cover, bring to the boil, remove the scum, cover the pan with a tight fitting lid and simmer for 1½ hours. Add the soy sauce, sherry, sugar, whole spring onions (scallions) and ginger cut into thin slices, bring back to simmering point; cover and cook for another 1 hour.

Serve the pork on a large dish with some of the liquid and pick pieces off with chopsticks or with a fork.

PORK WITH BEAN SPROUTS AND ALMONDS

IMPERIAL/METRIC	AMERICAN
¾ lb./375 g. shoulder of pork	¾ lb. shoulder of pork
1 lb./½ kg. bean sprouts	1 lb. bean sprouts
2 oz./60 g. blanched almonds	½ cup blanched almonds
1 tablespoon soy sauce	1 tablespoon soy sauce
2 tablespoons chicken stock	2 tablespoons chicken stock
1 teaspoon sugar	1 teaspoon sugar
2 tablespoons peanut oil	2 tablespoons peanut oil
2 spring onions, thinly sliced	2 scallions, thinly sliced
1 pineapple ring, chopped	1 pineapple ring, chopped
salt and pepper	salt and pepper

METHOD

Cut the pork into ½ inch cubes. Drain the bean sprouts, rinse in cold running water and drain again. Halve the almonds. Mix together the soy sauce, chicken stock and sugar.

Heat the oil in a frying pan (skillet) and fry the pork, stirring, until it changes colour. Add the almonds and spring onions (scallions) and fry for 3–4 minutes. Pour off any oil. Add all the other ingredients, including the bean sprouts. Combine thoroughly, cover the pan and cook for 2 minutes.

Pork and bean curd

PORK AND BEAN CURD

IMPERIAL/METRIC	AMERICAN
2 lb./1 kg. lean pork	2 lb. lean pork
4 tablespoons soy sauce	$\frac{1}{3}$ cup soy sauce
1 tablespoon sherry	1 tablespoon sherry
1 teaspoon brown sugar	1 teaspoon brown sugar
1 teaspoon salt	1 teaspoon salt
$\frac{1}{2}$ lb./250 g. bean curd	$\frac{1}{2}$ lb. bean curd
2 tablespoons oil	2 tablespoons oil
1 spring onion	1 scallion

METHOD

Wipe the pork, cut into small cubes and put into a pan with 1 pint ($\frac{1}{2}$ litre/2$\frac{1}{2}$ cups) water. Bring to the boil, remove the scum, cover the pan and simmer for 1 hour. Add half the soy sauce, all the sherry, sugar and salt. Cover and cook for another 30 minutes.

Cut the bean curd into 2 inch square pieces. Heat the oil and fry the bean curd for 2–3 minutes, turning it over once during cooking. Add the remaining soy sauce, $\frac{1}{2}$ pint ($\frac{1}{4}$ litre/1$\frac{1}{4}$ cups) water and the spring onion (scallion), cut into small pieces. Stir well and cook for 10 minutes, stirring occasionally. Mix the bean curd mixture into the pork and pour into a dish.

PORK AND MUSHROOMS

IMPERIAL/METRIC	AMERICAN
1 lb./½ kg. lean pork	1 lb. lean pork
1 tablespoon soy sauce	1 tablespoon soy sauce
1 tablespoon sherry	1 tablespoon sherry
2 tablespoons oil	2 tablespoons oil
4 oz./125 g. fresh mushrooms	4 oz. fresh mushrooms
1 teaspoon cornflour	1 teaspoon cornstarch
3 tablespoons stock or water	¼ cup stock or water

METHOD

Cut the pork into paper thin slices, add the soy sauce and sherry. Toss well. Heat the oil and fry the meat over fierce heat, stirring all the time, for 2 minutes. Remove from the pan and keep hot. Wash and dry the mushrooms. Slice them thinly and fry quickly in the remaining fat. Add the meat again and mix well.

Mix the cornflour (cornstarch) to a smooth paste with the stock or water, add to the pan and heat gently, stirring all the time, until slightly thickened.

PORK AND BROCCOLI

IMPERIAL/METRIC	AMERICAN
¾ lb./375 g. frozen broccoli	¾ lb. frozen broccoli
¾ lb./375 g. lean pork	¾ lb. lean pork
1 clove garlic, crushed	1 clove garlic, crushed
1 teaspoon salt	1 teaspoon salt
1 teaspoon brown sugar	1 teaspoon brown sugar
1 tablespoon soy sauce	1 tablespoon soy sauce
1 tablespoon sherry	1 tablespoon sherry
2 tablespoons oil	2 tablespoons oil
7 oz./200 g. canned crab meat	7 oz. canned crab meat
½ pint/¼ litre stock or water	1¼ cups stock or water
1 tablespoon cornflour	1 tablespoon cornstarch

METHOD

Defrost the broccoli and cut it into 1 inch lengths. Cut the meat into fine shreds. Add the garlic, salt, sugar, soy sauce and sherry to the meat, mix well and leave for 10 minutes. Heat the oil and fry the meat for 10 minutes over gentle heat, add the broccoli and cook for 2–3 minutes. Drain the crab and add to the pan, mix well.

Mix the cornflour (cornstarch) to a smooth paste with a little of the stock or water, then add the rest of the stock and add to the pan; bring to the boil, stirring until thickened.

SHREDDED SPICED PORK

IMPERIAL/METRIC	AMERICAN
1 lb./½ kg. lean pork	1 lb. lean pork
4 dried mushrooms	4 dried mushrooms
6 water chestnuts, sliced	6 water chestnuts, sliced
2 spring onions, chopped	2 scallions, chopped
1 egg	1 egg
2 oz./60 g. cornflour	½ cup cornstarch
oil for deep frying	oil for deep frying
1 tablespoon peanut oil	1 tablespoon peanut oil
1 teaspoon soy sauce	1 teaspoon soy sauce
2 teaspoons hoi sin sauce	2 teaspoons hoi sin sauce
¼ teaspoon cayenne pepper	¼ teaspoon cayenne pepper
½ teaspoon salt	½ teaspoon salt
1 oz./30 g. transparent noodles for garnish	1 oz. transparent noodles for garnish

METHOD

Cut the pork into thin slices. Soak mushrooms in warm water, rinse, squeeze dry and slice thinly, discarding the stalks.

Beat the egg and cornflour (cornstarch) together. Coat the pork in this batter and deep fry in hot oil until it is beginning to brown. Heat the peanut oil in a frying pan (skillet). Add the mushrooms, water chestnuts, spring onions (scallions), soy sauce, hoi sin sauce, cayenne pepper, salt and fried pork. Cook for 5 minutes, stirring constantly.

Fry noodles in deep hot oil for about 15 seconds. Serve pork on a heated dish, topped with the noodles.

Pork and mushrooms

PORK WITH MUSHROOMS AND CAULIFLOWER

IMPERIAL/METRIC	AMERICAN
2 lb./1 kg. pork chops	2 lb. pork chops
1 pint/½ litre water	2½ cups water
4 oz./125 g. dried mushrooms	4 oz. dried mushrooms
4 tablespoons soy sauce	⅓ cup soy sauce
3 tablespoons sherry	¼ cup sherry
4 spring onions	4 scallions
1 teaspoon brown sugar	1 teaspoon brown sugar
1 teaspoon salt	1 teaspoon salt
1 cauliflower	1 cauliflower

METHOD

Wipe the chops and put them in a large pan with the water. Bring to the boil, remove the scum, cover the pan with a tight fitting lid and simmer for 30 minutes.

Soak the mushrooms in hot water for 20 minutes, drain and chop finely. Add to the pan with the soy sauce, sherry, whole spring onions (scallions), sugar and salt. Cover and simmer for a further 45 minutes.

Wash the cauliflower and break it into florets. Add them to the pan, mix well and cook for a further 15 minutes.

Pork with mushrooms and cauliflower

RED PORK CHOPS

IMPERIAL/METRIC
2 lb./1 kg. pork chops
½ pint/¼ litre water
1 oz./30 g. fresh ginger
6 tablespoons soy sauce
2 tablespoons sherry
1 teaspoon salt
1 teaspoon brown sugar

AMERICAN
2 lb. pork chops
1¼ cups water
1 oz. fresh ginger
½ cup soy sauce
2 tablespoons sherry
1 teaspoon salt
1 teaspoon brown sugar

METHOD
Put the chops in a large saucepan with the water. Bring to the boil, remove the scum, cover the pan with a tight fitting lid (this is essential to prevent any evaporation of the small amount of liquid) and simmer very gently for about 1 hour. Shred the ginger and add to the pan with the rest of the ingredients; simmer for a further 30 minutes.

Pork and bamboo shoots

PORK AND BAMBOO SHOOTS

IMPERIAL/METRIC
2 lb./1 kg. lean pork
3 tablespoons soy sauce
1 tablespoon sherry
1 teaspoon brown sugar
1 teaspoon ground ginger
2 pints/1 litre water
4 oz./125 g. bamboo
 shoots

AMERICAN
2 lb. lean pork
¼ cup soy sauce
1 tablespoon sherry
1 teaspoon brown sugar
1 teaspoon ground ginger
5 cups water
4 oz. bamboo shoots

METHOD
Cut the pork into small cubes. Mix the soy sauce, sherry, sugar and ginger together, add to the pork, toss well and leave for 10 minutes.

Put pork and flavourings in a large pan, add the water and bring gently to the boil, cover and simmer for 1 hour. Drain bamboo shoots and shred finely, add to the pan and simmer for 10 minutes. If wished, liquid may be thickened with 1 tablespoon cornflour (cornstarch) mixed with a little cold water.

21

22

PORK WITH CHESTNUTS

IMPERIAL/METRIC	AMERICAN
2 lb./1 kg. lean pork	2 lb. lean pork
1 pint/½ litre water	2½ cups water
1 lb./½ kg. dried skinned chestnuts	1 lb. dried skinned chestnuts
4 tablespoons soy sauce	⅓ cup soy sauce
3 tablespoons sherry	¼ cup sherry
1 teaspoon brown sugar	1 teaspoon brown sugar
1 lb./½ kg. spinach	1 lb. spinach

METHOD

Cut the meat into small cubes. Put in a large pan with the water, bring to the boil, remove the scum, cover with a tight fitting lid and simmer for 1 hour.

Put the chestnuts in another large pan, cover with cold water, bring to the boil, cover and simmer for 1 hour. Drain the nuts, add to the pork with the soy sauce, sherry and brown sugar. Cook for 20 minutes.

Wash and drain the spinach. Put in a frying pan (skillet) with 2 tablespoons of the pork liquid. Cook quickly, stirring all the time for about 5 minutes. Put the spinach in a deep dish and pour the pork and liquid over the spinach.

CUCUMBER STUFFED PORK BALLS

IMPERIAL/METRIC	AMERICAN
½ lb./250 g. lean pork	½ lb. lean pork
1 egg	1 egg
1 teaspoon salt	1 teaspoon salt
2 tablespoons cornflour	2 tablespoons cornstarch
1 tablespoon sherry	1 tablespoon sherry
1 large cucumber	1 large cucumber
12 fresh mushrooms	12 fresh mushrooms
½ pint/¼ litre water	1¼ cups water
2 tablespoons soy sauce	2 tablespoons soy sauce

METHOD

Mince (grind) the pork finely, add the egg, salt, half the cornflour (cornstarch) and the sherry, beat well until evenly blended. Peel the cucumber and cut into twelve 2 inch lengths. Scoop out the seeds and pack the pork mixture into the centre of each one. Wash the mushrooms, remove the stalks and place a mushroom upside down over the pork mixture.

Stand the cucumber cups in a shallow pan, add the water, cover the pan and simmer gently for about 30 minutes. Lift the cucumber on to a hot dish. Keep hot.

Mix the remaining cornflour (cornstarch) to a smooth paste with the soy sauce and a little cold water, add to the remaining liquid in the pan and bring to the boil, stirring until slightly thickened. Pour over the cucumber.

PORK AND BEAN SPROUTS

IMPERIAL/METRIC	AMERICAN
¾ lb./375 g. pork tenderloin	¾ lb. pork tenderloin
2 teaspoons cornflour	2 teaspoons cornstarch
1 teaspoon brown sugar	1 teaspoon brown sugar
pinch of salt	pinch of salt
1 tablespoon soy sauce	1 tablespoon soy sauce
2 spring onions	2 scallions
1 tablespoon oil or melted lard	1 tablespoon oil or melted lard
1 lb./½ kg. bean sprouts	1 lb. bean sprouts
1 tablespoon oyster sauce	1 tablespoon oyster sauce
2 tablespoons stock or water	2 tablespoons stock or water

METHOD

Cut the pork into fine shreds, sprinkle with half the cornflour (cornstarch), sugar, salt and soy sauce. Mix well.

Chop the spring onions (scallions) finely and fry in the oil or lard for 1 minute. Add the pork and fry over fierce heat for 3 minutes, stirring all the time. Drain the bean sprouts and add to the pan; mix well and heat gently. Mix the remaining cornflour (cornstarch) with the oyster sauce and stock or water, add to the pan and bring to the boil, stirring until thickened.

Pork with chestnuts

RED ROAST PORK

IMPERIAL/METRIC	AMERICAN
1 lb./½ kg. pork fillet	1 lb. pork fillet
1 tablespoon hoi sin sauce	1 tablespoon hoi sin sauce
1 teaspoon five-spice powder	1 teaspoon five-spice powder
1 tablespoon soy sauce	1 tablespoon soy sauce
½ tablespoon soft brown sugar	½ tablespoon soft brown sugar
1 clove garlic, crushed	1 clove garlic, crushed
1 teaspoon very finely chopped fresh ginger	1 teaspoon very finely chopped fresh ginger
peanut oil	peanut oil

METHOD

Trim the pork but leave it in one piece. Mix together all the remaining ingredients except the oil and combine them thoroughly.

Place the meat in a dish, brush it with oil and then coat it in sauce. Marinate the pork for 1–2 hours. Spoon more oil over the pork, place on a rack in a roasting pan and roast in a hot oven (425°F/220°C, Mark 7) for 10 minutes. Reduce the oven temperature to moderate (350°F/180°C, Mark 4) for 30–35 minutes.

Cut the fillet in slices diagonally and serve on a hot plate.

NOTE: Other cuts of pork may be roasted with this sauce. Adjust the roasting time, allowing 35 minutes per pound.

PORK WITH CHICKEN AND VEGETABLES

IMPERIAL/METRIC	AMERICAN
½ lb./250 g. shoulder of pork	½ lb. shoulder of pork
4 oz./125 g. chicken	4 oz. chicken
1 small red pepper	1 small red pepper
1 onion	1 onion
2 sticks celery	2 sticks celery
6 water chestnuts	6 water chestnuts
5 oz./150 g. bamboo shoots	5 oz. bamboo shoots
2 oz./60 g. button mushrooms	2 oz. button mushrooms
2 tablespoons peanut oil	2 tablespoons peanut oil
1 tablespoon soy sauce	1 tablespoon soy sauce
¼ pint/1 dcl. chicken stock	¾ cup chicken stock
salt and pepper	salt and pepper
1 tablespoon cornflour	1 tablespoon cornstarch
4 oz./125 g. dried egg noodles	4 oz. dried egg noodles

METHOD

Cut the pork and the chicken into thin strips. Cut the pepper into matchstick strips and the onion into eighths. Slice the celery diagonally and the water chestnuts and bamboo shoots into thin slices. Wipe and slice the mushrooms.

Heat the oil in a saucepan and fry the pork and chicken until they change colour, stirring constantly. Add the vegetables and fry, stirring, for 2–3 minutes. Pour off excess oil. Add the soy sauce, stock and seasonings and simmer for 5–7 minutes. Mix the cornflour (cornstarch) with a little water, add to the pan and simmer, stirring, for 2–3 minutes.

Cook the noodles in boiling salted water for 15 minutes. Drain. Serve with sauce poured over the noodles.

PORK AND CUCUMBER

IMPERIAL/METRIC	AMERICAN
2 lb./1 kg. lean pork	2 lb. lean pork
1 pint/½ litre water	2½ cups water
3 tablespoons soy sauce	¼ cup soy sauce
2 tablespoons sherry	2 tablespoons sherry
1 teaspoon salt	1 teaspoon salt
pinch of ground ginger	pinch of ground ginger
1 large cucumber	1 large cucumber
2 tablespoons oil	2 tablespoons oil

METHOD

Wipe the meat and cut into small cubes. Put in a pan with the water. Bring to the boil, remove the scum, cover the pan with a tight fitting lid and simmer for 1 hour. Add the soy sauce, sherry, salt and ginger. Cook for another 30 minutes.

Peel the cucumber and cut into thin slices. Heat the oil and fry the cucumber for 3–4 minutes, stirring all the time. Pile the cucumber in a dish and pour the pork and some of the liquid over.

Red roast pork

*Sweet and sour pork
with lychees*

SWEET AND SOUR PORK WITH LYCHEES

IMPERIAL/METRIC	AMERICAN
1 lb./½ kg. shoulder of pork	1 lb. shoulder of pork
3 tablespoons soy sauce	¼ cup soy sauce
1 tablespoon dry sherry	1 tablespoon dry sherry
1 teaspoon very finely chopped fresh ginger	1 teaspoon very finely chopped fresh ginger
pinch of monosodium glutamate	pinch of monosodium glutamate
1 oz./30 g. plain flour	¼ cup all-purpose flour
1 oz./30 g. cornflour	¼ cup cornstarch
pinch of salt	pinch of salt
2 eggs, beaten	2 eggs, beaten
oil for deep frying	oil for deep frying
½ red pepper	½ red pepper
½ green pepper	½ green pepper
2 apples	2 apples
1 tablespoon brown sugar	1 tablespoon brown sugar
¼ pint/1 dcl. syrup from canned lychees	¾ cup syrup from canned lychees
2 tablespoons vinegar	2 tablespoons vinegar
4 spring onions, finely chopped	4 scallions, finely chopped
11 oz./325 g. canned lychees, drained	11 oz. canned lychees, drained
extra 1 tablespoon cornflour	extra 1 tablespoon cornstarch
extra 1 tablespoon soy sauce	extra 1 tablespoon soy sauce
salt to taste	salt to taste

METHOD

Cut the pork into 1 inch cubes. Mix together in a bowl the soy sauce, sherry, ginger and monosodium glutamate. Add the pork, stir to coat and marinate for 1–2 hours.

Sift the flour, cornflour (cornstarch) and salt into a bowl. Add the eggs gradually, beating well, to make a smooth batter. Coat the pork cubes in batter and deep fry in hot oil until golden. Drain on absorbent kitchen paper and keep hot. Cut the peppers into wedges. Peel, core and quarter the apples. Mix with all the remaining ingredients in a small saucepan. Bring to the boil, stirring constantly, and simmer for 2–3 minutes.

Put the pork on a heated serving dish and pour the sauce over.

CRISPY PORK

IMPERIAL/METRIC	AMERICAN
1 lb./½ kg. lean pork	1 lb. lean pork
2 tablespoons soy sauce	2 tablespoons soy sauce
1 tablespoon sugar	1 tablespoon sugar
1 clove star anise	1 clove star anise
1 tablespoon sherry (optional)	1 tablespoon sherry (optional)
pinch of monosodium glutamate	pinch of monosodium glutamate
4 oz./125 g. self-raising flour	1 cup self-rising flour
pinch of salt	pinch of salt
1 egg	1 egg
oil for frying	oil for frying

METHOD

Cut the pork into 1 inch cubes. Put them in a saucepan with ¾ pint (3½ dcl./2 cups) water, soy sauce, sugar, star anise, sherry and monosodium glutamate. Simmer until tender, about 45 minutes. Drain well.

Sift the flour and salt into a bowl. Make a well in the centre, drop in the egg and mix with a wooden spoon, gradually bringing in the flour from around the edge. Add ¼ pint (1 dcl./¾ cup) water gradually, beating continually. Add the pork pieces and stir to coat in batter.

Heat oil in a frying pan (skillet) and deep fry the coated pork pieces until crisp and golden. Drain well on absorbent kitchen paper.

Shredded lamb with onions;
Crispy pork

SHREDDED LAMB
WITH ONIONS

IMPERIAL/METRIC
1 lb./½ kg. lean lamb
  (shoulder or leg)
4 onions
1 clove garlic, crushed
1 tablespoon soy sauce
1 tablespoon dry sherry
¼ pint/1 dcl. chicken
  stock
1 tablespoon cornflour
1 teaspoon salt
2 tablespoons peanut oil

AMERICAN
1 lb. lean lamb (shoulder
  or leg)
4 onions
1 clove garlic, crushed
1 tablespoon soy sauce
1 tablespoon dry sherry
¾ cup chicken stock

1 tablespoon cornstarch
1 teaspoon salt
2 tablespoons peanut oil

METHOD
Cut the lamb into long thin strips. Slice the onions into
⅛ inch rounds. Mix together the garlic, soy sauce, sherry,
stock, cornflour (cornstarch) and salt.

   Heat the oil in a saucepan and fry the lamb until it
changes colour. Stir the cornflour (cornstarch) mixture
and add it to the pan with the onions. Bring to the boil,
stirring, and simmer for 2–3 minutes.

27

STEWED LAMB WITH ORANGE

IMPERIAL/METRIC	AMERICAN
2 lb./1 kg. lean lamb or mutton	2 lb. lean lamb or mutton
1 tablespoon soy sauce	1 tablespoon soy sauce
1 tablespoon sherry	1 tablespoon sherry
1 teaspoon ground ginger	1 teaspoon ground ginger
2 tablespoons finely grated orange rind	2 tablespoons finely grated orange rind
1 teaspoon salt	1 teaspoon salt
2 pints/1 litre stock or water	5 cups stock or water
1 tablespoon cornflour	1 tablespoon cornstarch

METHOD

Wipe the meat, then cut into $\frac{1}{2}$ inch cubes. Mix the soy sauce, sherry, ginger, orange rind and salt together, add to the lamb and mix well. Put the lamb into a pan with the flavourings and water. Bring to the boil, remove the scum, cover and simmer for 2 hours.

Mix the cornflour (cornstarch) to a smooth paste with a little cold water and add to the pan, bring back to the boil, stirring until slightly thickened.

BRAISED LAMB WITH VEGETABLES

IMPERIAL/METRIC	AMERICAN
$\frac{3}{4}$ lb./375 g. shoulder or leg of lamb	$\frac{3}{4}$ lb. shoulder or leg of lamb
1 egg	1 egg
2 tablespoons cornflour	2 tablespoons cornstarch
oil for deep frying	oil for deep frying
1 red pepper	1 red pepper
1 onion	1 onion
2 sticks celery	2 sticks celery
5 oz./150 g. bamboo shoots	5 oz. bamboo shoots
1 tablespoon soy sauce	1 tablespoon soy sauce
1 teaspoon hoi sin sauce	1 teaspoon hoi sin sauce
1 teaspoon very finely chopped fresh ginger	1 teaspoon very finely chopped fresh ginger
1 clove garlic, crushed	1 clove garlic, crushed
pinch of monosodium glutamate	pinch of monosodium glutamate
extra 1 tablespoon cornflour	extra 1 tablespoon cornstarch
salt	salt
$\frac{1}{4}$ pint/1 dcl. water	$\frac{3}{4}$ cup water

METHOD

Cut the lamb into thin strips, about 2 inches by $\frac{1}{4}$ inch by $\frac{1}{4}$ inch. Beat the egg and cornflour (cornstarch) together, add the lamb and stir to coat. Drain off any excess egg, then deep fry the meat until golden. Drain well on absorbent kitchen paper. Cut the pepper into wedges and the onion into eighths. Drop the pepper and onion into boiling water and cook for 5 minutes; drain. Slice the celery diagonally and the bamboo shoot into thin strips.

Mix together in a saucepan, the soy sauce, hoi sin sauce, ginger, garlic, monosodium glutamate, salt, the extra cornflour (cornstarch) and the water. Bring to the boil, stirring constantly, add the vegetables and simmer for 2–3 minutes. Add the lamb and reheat.

JELLIED LAMB

IMPERIAL/METRIC	AMERICAN
3 lb./1$\frac{1}{2}$ kg. leg of lamb	3 lb. leg of lamb
4 spring onions	4 scallions
1 teaspoon salt	1 teaspoon salt
4 tablespoons soy sauce	$\frac{1}{3}$ cup soy sauce

METHOD

Cut the lamb into small pieces and chop the bones up small. Chop the spring onions (scallions) and put into a large saucepan with the lamb, bones and salt. Cover with cold water and bring to the boil, remove the scum, add the soy sauce, cover the pan and simmer for 2$\frac{1}{2}$ hours.

Remove all the lamb bones and pick the meat into small pieces, put into a straight sided dish with some of the liquid and press down with a weight on top. Leave until cold and set.

Cut into slices to serve.

Stewed lamb with orange

LAMB WITH BEAN SPROUTS

IMPERIAL/METRIC
1 lb./½ kg. lean lamb
1 clove garlic
1 teaspoon salt
4 tablespoons soy sauce
pinch of ground ginger
1 teaspoon brown sugar
4 tablespoons oil
4 oz./125 g. bean sprouts
4 spring onions
1 tablespoon cornflour
¼ pint/1 dcl. water

AMERICAN
1 lb. lean lamb
1 clove garlic
1 teaspoon salt
⅓ cup soy sauce
pinch of ground ginger
1 teaspoon brown sugar
⅓ cup oil
4 oz. bean sprouts
4 scallions
1 tablespoon cornstarch
¾ cup water

METHOD
Cut the meat into thin slices; crush the garlic and add to the meat with the salt, soy sauce, ginger, sugar and oil. Mix well and cook gently for 3 minutes. Drain the bean sprouts, chop spring onions (scallions) and add to the pan; mix well and cook for 1 minute.

Mix the cornflour (cornstarch) to a smooth paste with the water, add to the pan and bring to the boil, stirring until slightly thickened.

LAMB WITH PEA SPROUTS AND SPRING ONIONS (SCALLIONS)

IMPERIAL/METRIC
1 lb./½ kg. lean lamb
1 tablespoon cornflour
3 spring onions
2 cloves garlic
2 tablespoons oil
1 teaspoon salt
4 oz./125 g. pea sprouts
1 tablespoon soy sauce
1 tablespoon sherry

AMERICAN
1 lb. lean lamb
1 tablespoon cornstarch
3 scallions
2 cloves garlic
2 tablespoons oil
1 teaspoon salt
4 oz. pea sprouts
1 tablespoon soy sauce
1 tablespoon sherry

METHOD
Cut the lamb into strips about 1½ inches long by ¼ inch thick. Toss in the cornflour (cornstarch). Cut the spring onions (scallions) into 1 inch lengths; crush the garlic.

Fry the meat in the oil and salt for 5 minutes, add the spring onions (scallions), crushed garlic, salt and pea sprouts, mix well and cook together for 1 minute. Add the soy sauce, sherry and 2 tablespoons water. Bring to the boil and mix well.

WOOLLY LAMB

IMPERIAL/METRIC	AMERICAN
1 lb./½ kg. leg or shoulder of lamb	1 lb. leg or shoulder of lamb
5 oz./150 g. bamboo shoots	5 oz. bamboo shoots
1 onion	1 onion
1 carrot	1 carrot
2 dried mushrooms	2 dried mushrooms
2 tablespoons peanut oil	2 tablespoons peanut oil
½ teaspoon salt	½ teaspoon salt
½ pint/¼ litre chicken stock	1¼ cups chicken stock
1 tablespoon soy sauce	1 tablespoon soy sauce
½ teaspoon sugar	½ teaspoon sugar
2 tablespoons cornflour	2 tablespoons cornstarch
2 oz./60 g. transparent noodles	2 oz. transparent noodles
oil for deep frying	oil for deep frying

METHOD

Cut the lamb into thin slices and the bamboo shoot into thin strips. Cut the onion into eighths and the carrot into wedges. Soak the mushrooms in warm water for 20 minutes, rinse, squeeze dry and slice; discard the stalks.

Heat the oil in a saucepan and fry the meat until it changes colour. Pour off the excess oil and add the prepared vegetables, salt, stock, soy sauce, sugar and cornflour (cornstarch). Bring to the boil and simmer, stirring constantly, for 5 minutes. Loosen the transparent noodles and deep fry in hot oil until they puff up, in about 15 seconds. Drain well on absorbent kitchen paper.

Serve the lamb mixture on a heated serving plate, topped with the noodles.

NOTE: This unusual dish owes its name and spectacular appearance to the transparent noodles. If these are not available, substitute 4 ounces/125 g. of Chinese egg noodles, which should be boiled in water for five minutes, drained and fried.

Woolly lamb

SPICED WHOLE LAMB

IMPERIAL/METRIC	AMERICAN
3 lb./1½ kg. leg or shoulder of lamb	3 lb. leg or shoulder of lamb
1 teaspoon salt	1 teaspoon salt
1 tablespoon soy sauce	1 tablespoon soy sauce
1 tablespoon sherry	1 tablespoon sherry
2 cloves garlic, crushed	2 cloves garlic, crushed
1 oz./30 g. fresh ginger, shredded, or 1 teaspoon ground ginger	1 oz. fresh ginger, shredded, or 1 teaspoon ground ginger
4 tablespoons oil	⅓ cup oil
2 pints/1 litre stock	5 cups stock
1 tablespoon cornflour	1 tablespoon cornstarch

METHOD

Wipe the meat and rub salt into the skin. Put in a pan with cold water to cover, bring to the boil, remove the scum, cover and simmer for 20 minutes. Drain off the liquid. Mix the soy sauce and sherry with the garlic and ginger and rub into the lamb; leave for 10 minutes.

Heat the oil and fry the lamb for about 15 minutes, turning it to brown all over. Add the stock, bring to the boil, cover and simmer for 2½ hours.

Mix the cornflour (cornstarch) to a smooth paste with a little cold water. Lift the lamb on to a hot dish; keep hot. Add cornflour (cornstarch) mixture to the liquid in the pan and bring to the boil, stirring, until slightly thickened. Pour over the lamb.

Spiced whole lamb

LAMB AND VERMICELLI (BEAN THREADS)

IMPERIAL/METRIC	AMERICAN
4 oz./125 g. vermicelli	4 oz. bean threads
½ lb./250 g. lean lamb	½ lb. lean lamb
1 teaspoon cornflour	1 teaspoon cornstarch
1 egg	1 egg
1 tablespoon oil	1 tablespoon oil
2 teaspoons soy sauce	2 teaspoons soy sauce
2 tablespoons tomato ketchup	2 tablespoons tomato catsup
1 tablespoon sherry	1 tablespoon sherry
pinch of salt	pinch of salt
pinch of black pepper	pinch of black pepper
3 spring onions	3 scallions
½ pint/¼ litre stock	1¼ cups stock

METHOD

Soak the vermicelli (bean threads) in hot water for 10 minutes. Cut the meat into strips about 1½ inches long by ¼ inch wide. Mix the cornflour (cornstarch) to a smooth paste with 1 tablespoon water, add the egg and beat well. Add to the lamb and toss to coat completely.

Heat the oil and fry the meat quickly, stirring all the time, for 2–3 minutes. Drain. Add the vermicelli (bean threads) to the pan, stir well and cook for 2–3 minutes. Mix the soy sauce, tomato ketchup (catsup), sherry, salt and pepper together, add to the vermicelli (bean threads) with the meat. Mix well. Chop the spring onions (scallions) finely, add to the pan, bring to the boil and cook for 1 minute. Add the stock and cook for 5 minutes.

Lamb and vermicelli (bean threads)

BEEF CHOW MEIN

IMPERIAL/METRIC	AMERICAN
¾ lb./375 g. topside or rump steak	¾ lb. round or rump steak
1 teaspoon salt	1 teaspoon salt
2 teaspoons sugar	2 teaspoons sugar
1 tablespoon soy sauce	1 tablespoon soy sauce
pinch of monosodium glutamate	pinch of monosodium glutamate
4 dried mushrooms	4 dried mushrooms
1 lb./½ kg. bean sprouts	1 lb. bean sprouts
2½ oz./75 g. bamboo shoots	2¼ oz. bamboo shoots
4 spring onions	4 scallions
2 tablespoons cornflour	2 tablespoons cornstarch
¾ pint/3½ dcl. beef stock	2 cups beef stock
3 tablespoons peanut oil	¼ cup peanut oil
4 oz./125 g. dried egg noodles	4 oz. dried egg noodles
oil for deep frying	oil for deep frying
1 egg, beaten	1 egg, beaten

METHOD

Cut the beef into strips, about 2 inches by ¼ inch by ¼ inch. Mix together in a bowl the salt, sugar, soy sauce and monosodium glutamate. Marinate the beef in this for 30 minutes.

Soak the mushrooms in warm water for 20 minutes, rinse, squeeze dry and slice, discarding the stalks. Drain the bean sprouts, rinse and drain again. Slice the bamboo shoots into thin strips. Cut the spring onions (scallions) into 1 inch lengths. Mix the cornflour (cornstarch) and stock together.

Drain the beef and reserve marinade. Heat the oil and fry the beef, stirring, for 3–4 minutes. Add the marinade and cornflour (cornstarch) mixture. Bring to the boil, stirring constantly, add the vegetables and simmer for 5 minutes.

Cook the noodles in boiling water for 5 minutes; drain thoroughly. Deep fry just before needed. Drain well on absorbent kitchen paper. Beat the egg with 1 tablespoon water and pour into a heated, lightly oiled omelet pan. Make a small omelet and cut into thin strips.

Place noodles on a heated serving dish, top with the beef mixture and garnish with strips of omelet.

HAM AND RED PEPPERS

IMPERIAL/METRIC	AMERICAN
3 red peppers	3 red peppers
¾ lb./375 g. ham	¾ lb. ham
1 tablespoon cornflour	1 tablespoon cornstarch
2 tablespoons soy sauce	2 tablespoons soy sauce
1 tablespoon sherry	1 tablespoon sherry
1 teaspoon sugar	1 teaspoon sugar
2 tablespoons stock or water	2 tablespoons stock or water
2 tablespoons oil	2 tablespoons oil

METHOD

Wash the peppers, core them, and cut the flesh into 1 inch pieces. Cover with boiling water for 1 minute; drain. Cut the ham into 1 inch squares. Mix the cornflour (cornstarch), soy sauce, sherry, sugar and stock or water, together, add to the ham and mix well so that the meat is completely coated.

Heat the oil and fry the pepper pieces for 2 minutes over fierce heat, stirring all the time. Remove from the pan. Add the ham to the pan with the liquid, cook for 1 minute, stirring all the time over medium heat. Add the peppers, cook together with the ham for a further minute.

Beef chow mein

Ham and red peppers

BEEF WITH CELERY AND CABBAGE

IMPERIAL/METRIC	AMERICAN
1 lb./½ kg. rump steak	1 lb. rump steak
1 teaspoon cornflour	1 teaspoon cornstarch
2 tablespoons oil or melted dripping	2 tablespoons oil or melted dripping
2 sticks celery	2 sticks celery
4 spring onions	4 scallions
4 oz./125 g. white cabbage	4 oz. white cabbage
1 tablespoon soy sauce	1 tablespoon soy sauce
pinch of salt	pinch of salt
pinch of black pepper	pinch of black pepper

METHOD

Wipe the meat and cut into paper thin slices. Mix the cornflour (cornstarch) to a smooth paste with about 2 tablespoons water, add to the beef and mix well until the beef is completely coated with the mixture. Heat the oil or dripping and fry the meat over fierce heat, stirring all the time, for 3 minutes. Remove the meat from the pan.

Wash and shred the celery; wash and finely chop the spring onions (scallions); wash and shred the cabbage. Add the vegetables to the remaining fat in the pan and fry gently for 5 minutes, stirring occasionally. Add the meat, soy sauce, salt and pepper, mix well and cook for 2–3 minutes.

MEAT BALLS WITH PINEAPPLE

IMPERIAL/METRIC	AMERICAN
½ lb./250 g. stewing steak	½ lb. chuck or blade steak
1 onion	1 onion
½ egg	½ egg
salt and pepper	salt and pepper
cornflour	cornstarch
oil for deep frying	oil for deep frying
7 oz./200 g. canned pineapple pieces	7 oz. canned pineapple pieces
¼ pint/1 dcl. syrup from canned pineapple	¾ cup syrup from canned pineapple
1 tablespoon cornflour	1 tablespoon cornstarch
2 tablespoons vinegar	2 tablespoons vinegar
1 tablespoon soy sauce	1 tablespoon soy sauce
2 tablespoons sugar	2 tablespoons sugar
green tops of 2 spring onions	green tops of 2 scallions

METHOD

Mince (grind) the steak and onion together. Beat the egg lightly and stir it into the meat. Season. Form the mixture into small balls and roll in cornflour (cornstarch). Deep fry them in hot oil until golden.

Place all the remaining ingredients in a saucepan and bring to the boil, stirring constantly. Add the meat balls and simmer, covered, for 5 minutes.

FRIED BEEF IN OYSTER SAUCE

IMPERIAL/METRIC	AMERICAN
1 lb./½ kg. rump steak	1 lb. rump steak
2 cloves garlic	2 cloves garlic
2 teaspoons cornflour	2 teaspoons cornstarch
1 tablespoon soy sauce	1 tablespoon soy sauce
1 tablespoon sherry	1 tablespoon sherry
pinch of salt	pinch of salt
pinch of black pepper	pinch of black pepper
1 tablespoon oil	1 tablespoon oil
1 tablespoon oyster sauce	1 tablespoon oyster sauce
6 tablespoons water	½ cup water

METHOD

Cut the meat into paper thin slices; crush the garlic. Mix the cornflour (cornstarch) to a smooth paste with the soy sauce, add the sherry, salt and pepper. Mix with the beef until all the meat is evenly coated.

Heat the oil with the garlic, then remove garlic from the oil and fry the beef over fierce heat for 2–3 minutes, stirring all the time. Add the oyster sauce, mix well and add the water. Cook for 1 minute.

Beef with celery and cabbage

SLICED BEEF WITH TOMATOES

IMPERIAL/METRIC	AMERICAN	METHOD
1 lb./½ kg. rump steak	1 lb. rump steak	Cut the meat into thin slices, add the egg and cornflour (cornstarch); mix well until coated. Heat the salt, oil and garlic, remove the garlic and fry the beef over fierce heat, stirring all the time, for 2 minutes. Remove from the pan.
1 egg	1 egg	
1 teaspoon cornflour	1 teaspoon cornstarch	
1 teaspoon salt	1 teaspoon salt	
2 tablespoons oil or melted lard	2 tablespoons oil or melted lard	Slice the tomatoes and fry in the remaining fat for 1 minute. Add the beef, tomato ketchup (catsup), sugar, soy sauce and sherry, mix well and bring to the boil. Mix well again.
1 clove garlic	1 clove garlic	
4 large tomatoes	4 large tomatoes	
1 tablespoon tomato ketchup	1 tablespoon tomato catsup	
1 teaspoon sugar	1 teaspoon sugar	
1 tablespoon soy sauce	1 tablespoon soy sauce	
1 tablespoon sherry	1 tablespoon sherry	

KIDNEY WITH SPRING ONIONS (SCALLIONS) AND CAULIFLOWER

IMPERIAL/METRIC	AMERICAN	METHOD
4 lamb's kidneys	4 lamb's kidneys	Wash and core the kidneys, slice them quickly, and soak in the sherry. Break the cauliflower into very small florets. Cook in salted boiling water for 3 minutes. Drain. Cut the spring onions (scallions) into 1 inch lengths.
2 tablespoons sherry	2 tablespoons sherry	
1 small cauliflower	1 small cauliflower	
4 spring onions	4 scallions	
2 tablespoons oil or melted lard	2 tablespoons oil or melted lard	Melt the lard and fry the kidneys and onions with the cauliflower for 2 minutes. Mix the cornflour (cornstarch) to a smooth paste with the soy sauce, 2 tablespoons water, the sugar, the remaining sherry and the salt. Add to the pan and cook gently for 3 minutes, stirring all the time.
1 tablespoon cornflour	1 tablespoon cornstarch	
1 tablespoon soy sauce	1 tablespoon soy sauce	
1 teaspoon brown sugar	1 teaspoon brown sugar	
1 teaspoon salt	1 teaspoon salt	

SHREDDED BEEF HEART

IMPERIAL/METRIC	AMERICAN	METHOD
1 lb./½ kg. beef or veal heart	1 lb. beef or veal heart	Trim the heart, removing all the tubes and blood vessels. Cut the flesh into very fine shreds and soak in cold water for 30 minutes. Drain. Add the soy sauce, sherry, sugar and salt to the heart, mix well. Mix the cornflour (cornstarch) to a smooth paste with the water, add to the heart, mix well.
2 tablespoons soy sauce	2 tablespoons soy sauce	
2 tablespoons sherry	2 tablespoons sherry	
1 teaspoon brown sugar	1 teaspoon brown sugar	
1 teaspoon salt	1 teaspoon salt	
1 tablespoon cornflour	1 tablespoon cornstarch	
2 tablespoons water	2 tablespoons water	Heat the oil or lard and fry the heart over fierce heat for 4–5 minutes, stirring all the time until browned. Chop the spring onions (scallions) and ginger, if fresh; add both to the beef and mix well.
3 tablespoons oil or melted lard	¼ cup oil or melted lard	
2 spring onions	2 scallions	
small pieces fresh ginger or 1 teaspoon ground ginger	small pieces fresh ginger or 1 teaspoon ground ginger	

LIVER AND SPRING ONIONS (SCALLIONS)

IMPERIAL/METRIC
1 lb./½ kg. lamb's liver
1 tablespoon cornflour
2 tablespoons sherry
2 tablespoons soy sauce
2 spring onions
2 leeks
2 tablespoons oil
1 teaspoon brown sugar
pinch of salt

AMERICAN
1 lb. lamb's liver
1 tablespoon cornstarch
2 tablespoons sherry
2 tablespoons soy sauce
2 scallions
2 leeks
2 tablespoons oil
1 teaspoon brown sugar
pinch of salt

METHOD
Wash and fry the liver, then cut into small slices 2 inches by ½ inch. Cover with boiling water for 1 minute. Drain. Mix the cornflour (cornstarch), sherry and soy sauce to a smooth paste, add to the liver and mix well. Chop the spring onions (scallions), wash and slice the leeks into 1 inch pieces.

Heat the oil and fry the liver for 1 minute over fierce heat, stirring all the time. Add the spring onions (scallions) and leeks, sugar and salt with any remaining cornflour (cornstarch) mixture. Heat quickly, stirring all the time, for 1 minute.

39

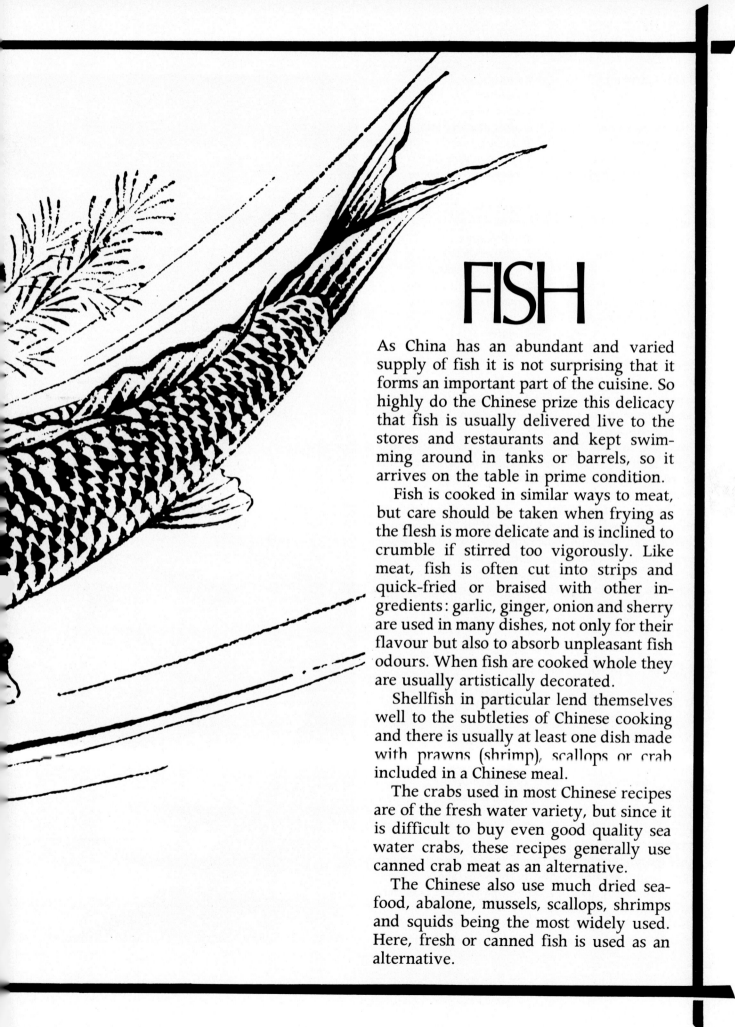

FISH

As China has an abundant and varied supply of fish it is not surprising that it forms an important part of the cuisine. So highly do the Chinese prize this delicacy that fish is usually delivered live to the stores and restaurants and kept swimming around in tanks or barrels, so it arrives on the table in prime condition.

Fish is cooked in similar ways to meat, but care should be taken when frying as the flesh is more delicate and is inclined to crumble if stirred too vigorously. Like meat, fish is often cut into strips and quick-fried or braised with other ingredients: garlic, ginger, onion and sherry are used in many dishes, not only for their flavour but also to absorb unpleasant fish odours. When fish are cooked whole they are usually artistically decorated.

Shellfish in particular lend themselves well to the subtleties of Chinese cooking and there is usually at least one dish made with prawns (shrimp), scallops or crab included in a Chinese meal.

The crabs used in most Chinese recipes are of the fresh water variety, but since it is difficult to buy even good quality sea water crabs, these recipes generally use canned crab meat as an alternative.

The Chinese also use much dried seafood, abalone, mussels, scallops, shrimps and squids being the most widely used. Here, fresh or canned fish is used as an alternative.

CRISP SKIN FISH

IMPERIAL/METRIC	AMERICAN
4 whiting	4 whiting
4 oz./125 g. prawns	4 oz. shrimp
4 dried mushrooms	4 dried mushrooms
1 spring onion	1 scallion
1 teaspoon very finely chopped fresh ginger	1 teaspoon very finely chopped fresh ginger
salt	salt
1 egg yolk	1 egg yolk
cornflour	cornstarch
oil for frying	oil for frying
1 tablespoon vinegar	1 tablespoon vinegar
1 tablespoon sugar	1 tablespoon sugar
2 tablespoons black beans	2 tablespoons black beans
1 tablespoon cornflour	1 tablespoon cornstarch
$\frac{1}{4}$ pint/1 dcl. fish stock or water	$\frac{3}{4}$ cup fish stock or water

METHOD

Clean the whiting, leaving on the heads and tails. Chop the peeled prawns (shrimp) and spring onions (scallions). Soak the mushrooms for 20 minutes, rinse, squeeze dry, and chop, discarding the stalks.

Mix the prawns (shrimp), mushrooms, onions and ginger; stuff each fish with this mixture and sew up. Rub salt into gashes cut on both sides of each fish.

Beat the egg yolk with 1 teaspoon water and brush over the fish. When nearly dry, rub over the cornflour (cornstarch). Fry the fish in 2 inches of oil, turning once. When cooked, drain on absorbent paper; keep hot. Place remaining ingredients in a saucepan with 1 tablespoon water and salt to taste. Bring to the boil, stirring, and simmer for 2–3 minutes. Place fish on a serving dish and pour the sauce over.

PRAWN (SHRIMP) FRITTERS

IMPERIAL/METRIC	AMERICAN
1 lb./$\frac{1}{2}$ kg. prawns	1 lb. shrimp
2 spring onions	2 scallions
1 egg	1 egg
5 tablespoons cornflour	$\frac{1}{2}$ cup cornstarch
$\frac{1}{2}$ pint/$\frac{1}{4}$ litre milk	$1\frac{1}{4}$ cups milk
$\frac{1}{2}$ teaspoon salt	$\frac{1}{2}$ teaspoon salt
deep fat for frying	deep fat for frying

METHOD

Mince (grind) the prawns (shrimp) twice; chop the spring onions (scallions) finely. Add both to the egg and cornflour (cornstarch), mix to a smooth paste, then gradually beat in the milk and add salt.

Drop tablespoons of the mixture into the hot fat and fry for 2–3 minutes, until golden brown, then drain.

WHITING WITH SOY SAUCE

IMPERIAL/METRIC	AMERICAN
3 whiting	3 whiting
2 tablespoons oil or melted lard	2 tablespoons oil or melted lard
1 teaspoon salt	1 teaspoon salt
pinch of black pepper	pinch of black pepper
2 tablespoons stock or water	2 tablespoons stock or water
3 tablespoons soy sauce	$\frac{1}{4}$ cup soy sauce
2 spring onions	2 scallions
$\frac{1}{2}$ teaspoon monosodium glutamate	$\frac{1}{2}$ teaspoon monosodium glutamate

METHOD

Clean the fish and remove the heads. Heat the oil and fry the fish on both sides for about 3 minutes, turning once during cooking. Add salt, pepper, stock or water and soy sauce, stir well and cook for 1 minute. Finely chop the spring onions (scallions), add to the pan and sprinkle with a pinch of monosodium glutamate.

FISH IN SWEET AND SOUR SAUCE

IMPERIAL/METRIC	AMERICAN
1 lb./$\frac{1}{2}$ kg. fish fillets	1 lb. fish fillets
1 carrot	1 carrot
1 green pepper	1 green pepper
2 sticks celery	2 sticks celery
3 tomatoes	3 tomatoes
3 tablespoons peanut oil	$\frac{1}{4}$ cup peanut oil
4 tablespoons vinegar	$\frac{1}{3}$ cup vinegar
4 tablespoons sugar	$\frac{1}{4}$ cup sugar
1 teaspoon very finely chopped fresh ginger	1 teaspoon very finely chopped fresh ginger
$\frac{1}{2}$ teaspoon salt	$\frac{1}{2}$ teaspoon salt
$\frac{1}{2}$ tablespoon cornflour (optional)	$\frac{1}{2}$ tablespoon cornstarch (optional)

METHOD

Skin the fish and cut it into bite-sized pieces. Cut the carrot and pepper into matchstick strips. Cut the celery diagonally. Drop the vegetables into boiling water and simmer for 5 minutes. Drain.

Skin the tomatoes, remove seeds and chop roughly. Heat the oil in a small pan and fry the fish until cooked, about 5–7 minutes. Remove the fish and drain.

·Pour off excess oil, add the vinegar, sugar, ginger, salt, cornflour (cornstarch), all the vegetables and $\frac{1}{4}$ pint (1 dcl./$\frac{3}{4}$ cup) water. Bring to the boil, stirring, add the fish and simmer for 2 minutes.

Crisp skin fish in preparation

SOLE WITH MUSHROOMS AND BAMBOO

IMPERIAL/METRIC	AMERICAN
1 tablespoon cornflour	1 tablespoon cornstarch
2 tablespoons soy sauce	2 tablespoons soy sauce
2 tablespoons sherry	2 tablespoons sherry
1 egg white	1 egg white
½ lb./250 g. sole fillets	½ lb. sole fillets
deep fat for frying	deep fat for frying
2 spring onions	2 scallions
2 oz./60 g. fresh mushrooms	2 oz. fresh mushrooms
2 oz./60 g. bamboo shoots	2 oz. bamboo shoots
1 small knob fresh ginger	1 small knob fresh ginger
2 tablespoons oil or lard	2 tablespoons oil or lard
2 tablespoons water	2 tablespoons water
½ teaspoon monosodium glutamate	½ teaspoon monosodium glutamate

METHOD

Mix the cornflour (cornstarch) to a smooth paste with a little of the soy sauce; add the rest with the sherry. Beat the egg white until smooth, then stir into the soy sauce mixture in a bowl.

Skin the fish and cut the flesh into strips about 1½ inches long. Toss in the soy sauce mixture and leave for 10 minutes. Fry the fish strips in deep fat for 2–3 minutes. Drain and keep hot.

Chop the spring onions (scallions) very finely; thinly slice the mushrooms; shred the bamboo shoots; shred the ginger. Heat the oil or lard and fry these ingredients for 1 minute over fierce heat. Stir well.

Mix the water with the remaining soy mixture, stir into the pan with the monosodium glutamate, heat gently, stirring until slightly thickened.

Pile the fish on a large serving dish and pour the vegetables over.

FISH ROLLS

IMPERIAL/METRIC	AMERICAN
1 lb./½ kg. thick fillet white fish (whiting, sole, halibut)	1 lb. thick fillet white fish (whiting, sole, halibut)
10 oz./300 g. canned asparagus tips	10 oz. canned asparagus tips
2 oz./60 g. minced ham or cooked pork	2 oz. ground ham or cooked pork
1 egg	1 egg
2 tablespoons cornflour	2 tablespoons cornstarch
deep fat for frying	deep fat for frying
1 spring onion	1 scallion
4 oz./125 g. mushrooms	4 oz. mushrooms
1 tablespoon soy sauce	1 tablespoon soy sauce

METHOD

Skin the fish and cut into fingers about 2½ inches by 1 inch. Make a slit through the centre to form a pocket. Drain the asparagus, keeping the liquid. Chop half the tips and mix with the ham. Press this mixture into each 'pocket'; secure with cocktail sticks.

Beat the egg and dip the fish in it, then in half the cornflour (cornstarch). Do this twice. Fry the fingers in hot deep fat for 4–5 minutes. Drain, remove sticks, and keep hot.

Chop the spring onions (scallions) very finely; wash and slice the mushrooms thinly; fry both in a little oil for 1 minute. Mix the rest of the cornflour (cornstarch) to a smooth paste with a little cold water, stir in soy sauce and 3–4 tablespoons of the asparagus liquid, mix well and add to the pan. Mix well. Add the remaining asparagus and heat gently, stirring until slightly thickened.

Arrange the vegetables on a large serving dish and place the fish rolls on top.

SHRIMPS WITH CHESTNUTS

IMPERIAL/METRIC	AMERICAN
2 pints/1 litre fish stock	5 cups fish stock
3 oz./90 g. dried shrimps	3 oz. dried shrimp
6 water chestnuts	6 water chestnuts
pinch of salt	pinch of salt
1 teaspoon brown sugar	1 teaspoon brown sugar
1 tablespoon soy sauce	1 tablespoon soy sauce
1 teaspoon sesame oil	1 teaspoon sesame oil

METHOD

Bring the stock to the boil, add the shrimps and simmer gently for 5 minutes.

Chop the water chestnuts roughly, add to the stock with the remaining ingredients. Bring back to the boil, then simmer for 2–3 minutes.

RAW FISH STRIPS

IMPERIAL/METRIC
1 lb./½ kg. plaice or
* salmon fillets*
1 spring onion
1 tablespoon sesame oil
2 tablespoons sherry
2 tablespoons soy sauce
pinch of salt
pinch of black pepper
1 slice pineapple

AMERICAN
1 lb. flounder or salmon
* fillets*
1 scallion
1 tablespoon sesame oil
2 tablespoons sherry
2 tablespoons soy sauce
pinch of salt
pinch of black pepper
1 slice pineapple

METHOD
Skin the fish and cut into narrow strips about 2 inches long.

Chop the spring onion (scallion) very finely and put into a shallow dish with the remaining ingredients, except the pineapple. Add the fish and toss well in the mixture. Leave for 10 minutes.

Lift the fish out of the mixture. Shred the pineapple very finely and mix with the fish.

Raw fish strips

Plaice (flounder) with vegetables and almonds

PLAICE (FLOUNDER) WITH VEGETABLES AND ALMONDS

IMPERIAL/METRIC
1 lb./½ kg. plaice fillets
1 egg
1 tablespoon flour
6 tablespoons oil or
   melted lard
4 oz./125 g. fresh mushrooms
4 spring onions
4 oz./125 g. bean sprouts
1 teaspoon cornflour
1 tablespoon water or
   stock
1 teaspoon sugar
2 tablespoons soy sauce
3 oz./90 g. sliced almonds,
   browned

AMERICAN
1 lb. flounder fillets
1 egg
1 tablespoon flour
½ cup oil or melted lard

4 oz. fresh mushrooms
4 scallions
4 oz. bean sprouts
1 teaspoon cornstarch
1 tablespoon water or
   stock
1 teaspoon sugar
2 tablespoons soy sauce
3 oz. sliced almonds,
   toasted

METHOD
Cut the fish into 2 inch strips, dip in beaten egg, then in flour; do this twice. Heat the oil or lard and fry the fish for 5 minutes. Drain and keep hot.

Wash and slice the mushrooms; chop the spring onions (scallions) finely; wash and drain the bean sprouts. Add all the vegetables to the remaining oil or lard and fry over fierce heat for 2–3 minutes, stirring all the time.

Mix the cornflour (cornstarch) to a smooth paste with the water or stock, add the sugar and soy sauce. Stir into the vegetables and heat gently until slightly thickened.

Pile the vegetables and their sauce on a large dish, arrange the fish on top and sprinkle with the almonds.

HONG KONG PLAICE (FLOUNDER)

IMPERIAL/METRIC	AMERICAN
3 spring onions	3 scallions
1 stick celery	1 stick celery
2 oz./60 g. water chestnuts	2 oz. water chestnuts
2 inch piece cucumber	2 inch piece cucumber
2 oz./60 g. fresh mushrooms	2 oz. fresh mushrooms
2 oz./60 g. bamboo shoots	2 oz. bamboo shoots
1 tablespoon oil	1 tablespoon oil
¼ pint/1 dcl. fish stock or water	¾ cup fish stock or water
½ lb./250 g. plaice fillets	½ lb. flounder fillets
1 tablespoon sherry	1 tablespoon sherry
pinch of black pepper	pinch of black pepper
1 teaspoon cornflour	1 teaspoon cornstarch
1 tablespoon water	1 tablespoon water
1 tablespoon soy sauce	1 tablespoon soy sauce

METHOD

Wash and finely chop the spring onions (scallions); shred the celery; thinly slice the chestnuts and cucumber; chop the mushrooms and shred the bamboo shoots. Heat the oil in a shallow pan, add the vegetables and fry over fierce heat for 2–3 minutes, stirring all the time. Add the stock or water, bring to the boil and simmer for 1 minute. Remove to a hot plate.

Cut the fish into strips about 2 inches long. Put in a greased pan with the sherry and pepper and add the vegetables. Mix the cornflour (cornstarch) to a smooth paste with the water and soy sauce, add to the pan and stir over low heat until slightly thickened.

BASS WITH GINGER

IMPERIAL/METRIC	AMERICAN
2 lb./1 kg. bass	2 lb. bass
2 teaspoons salt	2 teaspoons salt
1 small knob fresh ginger	1 small knob fresh ginger
2 spring onions	2 scallions
1 tablespoon soy sauce	1 tablespoon soy sauce
1 teaspoon oil	1 teaspoon oil

METHOD

Wash and clean the fish, removing the scales and fins. Put in a deep pan with the salt, cover with cold water and bring gently to the boil; cover and simmer for 5 minutes.

Wash and finely chop the ginger or use ground ginger if fresh is not available. Chop the spring onions (scallions) very finely, mix with the ginger, soy sauce and oil.

Lift the fish from the pan, drain and place on a large serving dish. Pour the ginger mixture over.

SESAME FISH

IMPERIAL/METRIC	AMERICAN
1 lb./½ kg. fish fillets	1 lb. fish fillets
1 teaspoon very finely chopped fresh ginger	1 teaspoon very finely chopped fresh ginger
1 onion	1 onion
2 tablespoons dry sherry	2 tablespoons dry sherry
½ teaspoon salt	½ teaspoon salt
pinch of pepper	pinch of pepper
1 teaspoon sugar	1 teaspoon sugar
1 oz./30 g. cornflour	1 oz. cornstarch
1 oz./30 g. plain flour	1 oz. all-purpose flour
1 egg	1 egg
sesame seeds	sesame seeds
oil for deep frying	oil for deep frying

METHOD

Skin the fish and cut into bite-sized pieces. Chop the onion finely and mix together in a bowl with the ginger, sherry, salt, pepper and sugar. Add the fish pieces and marinate for 10 minutes, stirring occasionally. Drain.

Sift the cornflour (cornstarch) and flour into a bowl. Add egg, 3 tablespoons water and mix well. Dip fish in this batter, then in sesame seeds. Deep fry in hot oil until crisp and golden.

SWEET AND SOUR FISH SLICES

IMPERIAL/METRIC	AMERICAN	METHOD
3 tomatoes	3 tomatoes	Skin and slice the tomatoes, mix with the pickle. Melt the lard and fry the tomatoes and pickle for 5 minutes. Mix the cornflour (cornstarch) to a smooth paste with the vinegar. Add the sugar, soy sauce and stock. Add to the tomato mixture, bring gently to the boil, stirring, until slightly thickened.
1 tablespoon sweet pickle	1 tablespoon sweet pickle	
1 oz./30 g. lard	1 oz. lard	
1 tablespoon cornflour	1 tablespoon cornstarch	
2 tablespoons vinegar	2 tablespoons vinegar	
2 tablespoons sugar	2 tablespoons sugar	
2 tablespoons soy sauce	2 tablespoons soy sauce	
¼ pint/1 dcl. bone stock	¾ cup bone stock	Cut the fish into 2 inch strips. Beat the egg and coat the fish with it, then dip fish in flour; do this twice. Fry the fish in deep fat for about 5 minutes, drain and pile on a serving dish. Pour the sauce over.
1 lb./½ kg. white fish fillets (whiting, sole, halibut)	1 lb. white fish fillets (whiting, sole, halibut)	
1 egg	1 egg	
2 tablespoons plain flour	2 tablespoons all-purpose flour	
deep fat for frying	deep fat for frying	

FISH BALLS

IMPERIAL/METRIC	AMERICAN	METHOD
1 lb./½ kg. white fish (whiting, sole, halibut)	1 lb. white fish (whiting, sole, halibut)	Skin and bone the fish; chop the flesh finely. Beat the egg and add to the fish with the cornflour (cornstarch); beat well until smooth and evenly blended.
1 egg	1 egg	
3 oz./90 g. cornflour	⅔ cup cornstarch	Put the fish stock, lemon juice and oil in a shallow pan, bring to the boil. Chop the spring onions (scallions) and crush the garlic, add to the stock, bring back to the boil.
¼ pint/1 dcl. fish stock	¾ cup fish stock	
1 tablespoon lemon juice	1 tablespoon lemon juice	
1 tablespoon oil	1 tablespoon oil	
2 spring onions	2 scallions	Shape the fish mixture into small balls, each the size of a pigeon's egg. Lower the fish balls, a few at a time, into the stock, and cook gently for about 5 minutes. Lift out and drain.
1 clove garlic	1 clove garlic	

BRAISED EEL

IMPERIAL/METRIC	AMERICAN	METHOD
1 lb./½ kg. eel	1 lb. eel	Skin the eel and cut into 2 inch lengths. Wash well and fry in the oil or lard for 5 minutes. Chop the spring onions (scallions) finely, add to the eel and fry gently for another 5 minutes. Crush the garlic, add to the pan with the sherry, soy sauce, sugar and salt, mix well, then add the water. Bring gently to the boil, cover and simmer for 15 minutes.
4 tablespoons oil or melted lard	⅓ cup oil or melted lard	
2 spring onions	2 scallions	
2 cloves garlic	2 cloves garlic	
2 tablespoons sherry	2 tablespoons sherry	
2 tablespoons soy sauce	2 tablespoons soy sauce	
1 teaspoon sugar	1 teaspoon sugar	Mix the cornflour (cornstarch) to a smooth paste with a little cold water, add to the pan, stir until slightly thickened.
½ teaspoon salt	½ teaspoon salt	
½ pint/¼ litre water	1¼ cups water	
1 teaspoon cornflour	1 teaspoon cornstarch	

Pineapple fish

PINEAPPLE FISH

IMPERIAL/METRIC	AMERICAN
1 lb./½ kg. haddock fillet, or 14 oz./435 g. canned tuna	1 lb. haddock or red snapper fillet, or 14 oz. canned tuna
4 oz./125 g. self-raising flour	1 cup self-rising flour
pinch of salt	pinch of salt
1 egg	1 egg
¼ pint/¼ litre water	1¼ cups water
pinch of monosodium glutamate	pinch of monosodium glutamate
4 pineapple rings	4 pineapple rings
2 tablespoons soft brown sugar	2 tablespoons soft brown sugar
1 tablespoon cornflour	1 tablespoon cornstarch
2 tablespoons vinegar	2 tablespoons vinegar
1 tablespoon soy sauce	1 tablespoon soy sauce
1 teaspoon very finely chopped fresh ginger	1 teaspoon very finely chopped fresh ginger
¼ pint/1 dcl. syrup from canned pineapple	¾ cup syrup from canned pineapple
salt to taste	salt to taste
browned flaked almonds	toasted flaked almonds
oil for deep frying	oil for deep frying

METHOD

Skin the fish and cut into bite-sized pieces or drain the tuna and break into bite-sized pieces.

Sift the flour and salt together in a mixing bowl. Make a well in the centre, add the egg and mix with a little of the flour, using a wooden spoon. Gradually add half the water and draw in the flour; beat until the batter is smooth. Beat in the monosodium glutamate.

Chop the pineapple roughly. Mix together the brown sugar, cornflour (cornstarch), vinegar, soy sauce, ginger, pineapple syrup, salt and the remaining water. Bring to the boil, stirring, and boil for 2–3 minutes.

Dip the fish pieces in batter and fry in deep hot oil until crisp and golden. Drain on absorbent kitchen paper. Add the pineapple pieces to the sauce and reheat.

Sprinkle the fish with the almonds and serve in a hot bowl with the sauce poured over.

SPLASHED FISH

IMPERIAL/METRIC
1 lb./½ kg. sprats
2 tablespoons oil
2 tablespoons soy sauce
2 tablespoons sherry
1 teaspoon salt
4 tablespoons water or
*   stock*
2 spring onions
1 small knob fresh ginger

AMERICAN
1 lb. sprats
2 tablespoons oil
2 tablespoons soy sauce
2 tablespoons sherry
1 teaspoon salt
⅓ cup water or stock

2 scallions
1 small knob fresh ginger

METHOD
Clean the fish and remove the heads. Fry in hot oil for 2–3 minutes. Drain and keep hot.

Add the soy sauce, sherry, salt, and stock or water to the remaining oil, and heat until boiling. Chop the spring onions (scallions) finely; shred the ginger; add to the pan and cook for 1 minute, then pour over the fish.

ABALONE AND CELERY

IMPERIAL/METRIC	AMERICAN
2 cans abalone	2 cans abalone
1 head celery	1 head celery
2 tablespoons soy sauce	2 tablespoons soy sauce
1 tablespoon brown sugar	1 tablespoon brown sugar
1 tablespoon salt	1 tablespoon salt
black pepper	black pepper
1 tablespoon sesame oil or nut oil	1 tablespoon sesame oil or nut oil

METHOD

Drain the abalone, keeping the juice for soup. Cut the abalone into fine shreds.

Wash the celery and cut into 1 inch pieces. Put in a pan of cold water, bring to the boil, simmer for 1 minute, then drain. Freshen under cold running water. Drain and mix with the abalone.

Mix the remaining ingredients together in a bowl. Add abalone mixture, toss well and serve cold.

GOLDEN BRAISED FISH

IMPERIAL/METRIC	AMERICAN
1 × 2 lb./1 kg. whole fish (bream or bass are suitable)	1 × 2 lb. whole fish (bass or red snapper are suitable)
salt	salt
plain flour	all-purpose flour
4 dried mushrooms	4 dried mushrooms
4 spring onions	4 scallions
oil for frying	oil for frying
1 teaspoon very finely chopped fresh ginger	1 teaspoon very finely chopped fresh ginger
$\frac{1}{2}$ pint/$\frac{1}{4}$ litre fish stock or water	$1\frac{1}{4}$ cups fish stock or water
2 tablespoons soy sauce	2 tablespoons soy sauce
1 tablespoon sherry	1 tablespoon sherry
1 teaspoon salt	1 teaspoon salt
6 water chestnuts	6 water chestnuts
2 cloves garlic, crushed	2 cloves garlic, crushed
1 clove star anise	1 clove star anise
1 teaspoon sugar	1 teaspoon sugar

METHOD

Clean the fish, leaving on the head and tail. Wipe inside and out with kitchen paper. Make 2 gashes on each side, in the thickest part. Sprinkle with salt and coat in flour. Soak the mushrooms in warm water for 20 minutes, rinse, squeeze dry and discard stalks. Cut the mushrooms into strips and the spring onions (scallions) into $\frac{1}{2}$ inch lengths. Slice the water chestnuts.

Heat a little oil in a large frying pan (skillet) and, when hot, fry the fish on both sides until golden. Pour off excess oil and add the mushrooms, spring onions (scallions), ginger, stock, soy sauce, sherry, salt, water chestnuts, garlic, star anise and sugar. Cover the pan, bring to the boil and simmer for about 30 minutes, turning the fish once.

Serve on a large heated platter with the sauce poured over.

Golden braised fish

FISH ROLLS WITH WALNUTS

IMPERIAL/METRIC	AMERICAN
2 large fish fillets (John Dory, plaice or sole)	*2 large fish fillets (flounder or sole)*
2 spring onions	*2 scallions*
¼ teaspoon salt	*¼ teaspoon salt*
¼ teaspoon sugar	*¼ teaspoon sugar*
½ teaspoon cornflour	*½ teaspoon cornstarch*
1 teaspoon soy sauce	*1 teaspoon soy sauce*
1 teaspoon dry sherry	*1 teaspoon dry sherry*
1 egg	*1 egg*
2 oz./60 g. walnuts, very finely chopped or ground	*½ cup walnuts, very finely chopped or ground*
2 × 1 oz./30 g. slices cooked ham	*2 × 1 oz. slices cooked ham*
8 wooden cocktail sticks	*8 wooden cocktail sticks*
oil for deep frying	*oil for deep frying*

METHOD

Cut the fillets into quarters, making 8 even-sized pieces. Chop the spring onions (scallions) finely, mix with salt, sugar, cornflour (cornstarch), soy sauce, sherry and egg and beat together well.

Dip the fish pieces in the egg mixture and then in the walnuts. Cut each slice of ham in quarters and lay a quarter on each piece of fish. Roll up and secure with a cocktail stick. Deep fry in hot oil until golden. Drain well on absorbent kitchen paper.

NOTE: This dish makes an ideal appetizer, either to begin the meal or served with drinks beforehand.

SCALLOPS WITH PEPPERS

IMPERIAL/METRIC	AMERICAN
1 lb./½ kg. scallops	*1 lb. scallops*
2 spring onions	*2 scallions*
1 tablespoon oil or melted lard	*1 tablespoon oil or melted lard*
1 teaspoon salt	*1 teaspoon salt*
2 red peppers	*2 red peppers*

METHOD

Wash and trim the scallops. Cut each into slices. Chop the spring onions (scallions) finely. Heat the oil or lard and fry the scallops and onions for about 3 minutes, stirring. Add the salt, mix well. Wash the peppers and cut into 1 inch pieces. Add to the pan with 4 tablespoons (⅓ cup) water and bring to the boil, stirring. Simmer for about 2 minutes.

Fish rolls with walnuts

PRAWNS (SHRIMP) WITH VEGETABLES

IMPERIAL/METRIC	AMERICAN
1 lb./½ kg. prawns, peeled	1 lb. shrimp, peeled
1 red pepper	1 red pepper
2 sticks celery	2 sticks celery
2 dried mushrooms	2 dried mushrooms
2 spring onions	2 scallions
6 water chestnuts	6 water chestnuts
1 tablespoon cornflour	1 tablespoon cornstarch
1 tablespoon soy sauce	1 tablespoon soy sauce
pinch of sugar	pinch of sugar
1 tablespoon peanut oil	1 tablespoon peanut oil
½ teaspoon very finely chopped fresh ginger	½ teaspoon very finely chopped fresh ginger
1 clove garlic, crushed	1 clove garlic, crushed
½ teaspoon salt	½ teaspoon salt
2 pineapple rings, chopped (optional)	2 pineapple rings, chopped (optional)
½ pint/¼ litre chicken stock	1¼ cups chicken stock
1 oz./30 g. flaked browned almonds	¼ cup flaked toasted almonds

METHOD

Prepare the prawns (shrimp). If using large prawns (shrimp), devein them and cut them in half.

Cut the pepper in matchstick strips and slice the celery diagonally. Soak the mushrooms in warm water for 20 minutes, rinse and squeeze dry, discard the stalks, and slice. Cut the spring onions (scallions) in ½ inch pieces and slice the water chestnuts. Mix the cornflour (cornstarch) with soy sauce, sugar and 2 tablespoons water.

Heat the oil and add the ginger, garlic and salt. Add the prepared vegetables, pineapple and stock. Bring to the boil and simmer, stirring, for 5 minutes. Add the cornflour (cornstarch) mixture and cook, stirring, for 2–3 minutes. Add the prawns and allow just to heat through. Scatter with the almonds.

PRAWN (SHRIMP) BALLS

IMPERIAL/METRIC	AMERICAN
4 oz./125 g. self-raising flour	1 cup self-rising flour
1 egg	1 egg
¼ pint/1 dcl. water	¾ cup water
pinch of salt	pinch of salt
1 lb./½ kg. peeled king prawns	1 lb. peeled king shrimp
2 tablespoons cornflour	2 tablespoons cornstarch
½ teaspoon salt	½ teaspoon salt
½ teaspoon white pepper	½ teaspoon white pepper
pinch of monosodium glutamate	pinch of monosodium glutamate
peanut oil for deep frying	peanut oil for deep frying
parsley sprigs for garnish	parsley sprigs for garnish

METHOD

Sift the flour and salt into a bowl. Make a well in the centre and add the egg. Using a wooden spoon, mix the flour into the egg, add half the water and continue mixing, drawing in the flour. Beat thoroughly and stir in remaining water. Cut the prawns (shrimp) into chunks about 1 inch across. Mix the cornflour (cornstarch) with the remaining salt, pepper and monosodium glutamate. Coat the prawn (shrimp) pieces in seasoned cornflour (cornstarch). Dip the prawns (shrimp) in batter and fry in deep, hot oil until crisp and golden. Drain well on absorbent kitchen paper. Garnish with sprigs of parsley.

NOTE: This dish may alternatively be served with a sweet and sour sauce.

Prawn (shrimp) balls

PRAWN (SHRIMP) CUTLETS

IMPERIAL/METRIC	AMERICAN
8 Mediterranean prawns	4 Pacific shrimp
1 tablespoon sherry	1 tablespoon sherry
1 egg	1 egg
2 tablespoons cornflour	2 tablespoons cornstarch
deep fat for frying	deep fat for frying

METHOD

Hold the prawns (shrimp) firmly by the tail and remove the rest of the shell, leaving the tail piece intact. Split the prawns (shrimp) in half lengthways almost to the tail and remove the intestinal cord. Flatten the prawns (shrimp) to look like cutlets. Sprinkle with sherry.

Beat the egg and dip the cutlets in it, then in the cornflour (cornstarch). Do this twice. Fry the cutlets in deep fat for 2–3 minutes. Drain and serve plain or with a sweet and sour sauce.

PRAWN (SHRIMP) CHOP SUEY

IMPERIAL/METRIC	AMERICAN
½ lb./250 g. peeled prawns	2 cups peeled shrimp
4 dried mushrooms	4 dried mushrooms
1 lb./½ kg. bean sprouts	1 lb. bean sprouts
4 oz./125 g. bamboo shoots	4 oz. bamboo shoots
8 water chestnuts	8 water chestnuts
½ tablespoon cornflour	½ tablespoon cornstarch
pinch of salt	pinch of salt
1 tablespoon soy sauce	1 tablespoon soy sauce
1 clove garlic, crushed	1 clove garlic, crushed
1 teaspoon sugar	1 teaspoon sugar
1 tablespoon dry sherry	1 tablespoon dry sherry
2 oz./60 g. browned almonds	½ cup toasted almonds

METHOD

Prepare the prawns (shrimp), cutting the large ones in half. Soak the mushrooms in warm water for 20 minutes, rinse, squeeze dry and slice, discarding the stalks. Rinse the bean sprouts under running cold water. Drain. Cut the bamboo shoots and water chestnuts into matchstick strips.

Mix the cornflour (cornstarch), salt, soy sauce, garlic, sugar, sherry, vegetables and 4 tablespoons water in a small saucepan. Bring to the boil and simmer slowly, stirring, for 2–3 minutes. Stir in the prawns (shrimp), cover the pan and reheat gently. Serve on a heated dish topped with the almonds.

SWEET AND SOUR PRAWNS (SHRIMP)

IMPERIAL/METRIC	AMERICAN
½ lb./250 g. peeled prawns	½ lb. peeled shrimp
1 tablespoon sherry	1 tablespoon sherry
salt and pepper	salt and pepper
1 onion	1 onion
1 green pepper	1 green pepper
1 tablespoon peanut oil	1 tablespoon peanut oil
½ lb./250 g. canned pineapple chunks	½ lb. canned pineapple chunks
1 tablespoon cornflour	1 tablespoon cornstarch
1 tablespoon soy sauce	1 tablespoon soy sauce
¼ pint/1 dcl. vinegar	¾ cup vinegar
4 tablespoons brown sugar	⅓ cup brown sugar

METHOD

Place the prawns (shrimp) in a bowl with the sherry and seasonings and marinate for 1 hour.

Slice the onion and cut the pepper into wedges. Put the oil in a small saucepan, add the vegetables, and fry gently until softened. Add the pineapple.

Mix together the cornflour (cornstarch), soy sauce, vinegar and sugar and add these to the saucepan. Bring to the boil, stirring constantly, and simmer for 2–3 minutes. Add the prawns (shrimp) and sherry and reheat.

Prawn (shrimp) cutlets

Crab with black beans

CRAB WITH BLACK BEANS

IMPERIAL/METRIC	AMERICAN
14 oz./435 g. canned crab meat	14 oz. canned crab meat
1 oz./30 g. black beans	1 oz. black beans
1 clove garlic	1 clove garlic
2 teaspoons sherry	2 teaspoons sherry
2 teaspoons oil	2 teaspoons oil
pinch of ground ginger	pinch of ground ginger

METHOD

Drain the crab and chop the meat finely. Arrange it in the base of a greased shallow dish or soufflé dish.

Put the beans in boiling water, bring them back to the boil, then drain and cool under cold running water. Mash them with a fork. Crush the garlic and mix with the beans, sherry, oil and ginger. Beat well to make a smooth paste. Spread this mixture over the crab. Cover the dish. Steam gently for 45 minutes.

Serve from the bowl.

NOTE: The correct way to eat any solid dish like this is to pinch out pieces from the dish with chopsticks – Westerners usually find a fork easier.

CRAB KROMESKIES WITH SWEET AND SOUR SAUCE

IMPERIAL/METRIC	AMERICAN
1 lb./½ kg. fresh crab meat	1 lb. fresh crab meat
2 spring onions	2 scallions
2 oz./60 g. fresh mushrooms	2 oz. fresh mushrooms
2 teaspoons oyster sauce	2 teaspoons oyster sauce
2 teaspoons soy sauce	2 teaspoons soy sauce
1 tablespoon sherry	1 tablespoon sherry
2 eggs	2 eggs
2 tablespoons cornflour	2 tablespoons cornstarch
deep fat for frying	deep fat for frying

METHOD

Chop the crab meat finely; wash and finely chop the spring onions (scallions); wash and chop the mushrooms. Mix these ingredients with the oyster and soy sauces, sherry and 1 egg. Beat well until smooth. Form into cork shapes.

Beat the remaining egg and dip the corks in it, then in the cornflour (cornstarch). Do this twice. Fry a few at a time in the hot fat for 4–5 minutes.

HONG KONG CRAB

IMPERIAL/METRIC	AMERICAN
4 tablespoons oil	⅓ cup oil
1 clove garlic	1 clove garlic
4 oz./125 g. lean pork	4 oz. lean pork
½ teaspoon salt	½ teaspoon salt
14 oz./435 g. canned crab meat	14 oz. canned crab meat
3 tablespoons soy sauce	¼ cup soy sauce
pinch of salt	pinch of salt
pinch of black pepper	pinch of black pepper
½ pint/¼ litre pork stock	1¼ cups pork stock
2 teaspoons cornflour	2 teaspoons cornstarch
1 egg	1 egg
2 spring onions	2 scallions

METHOD

Heat the oil, crush the garlic and fry for 1 minute. Mince (grind) the pork finely and add to the pan; fry for 4–5 minutes. Season with salt.

Drain the crab and cut the flesh into 1 inch pieces, add to the pan, mixing well. Cover and cook over gentle heat for 5 minutes. Add the soy sauce, salt, pepper, and stock; bring gently to the boil.

Mix the cornflour (cornstarch) to a smooth paste with a little cold water and add to the pan, stirring until slightly thickened. Beat the egg and pour in a thin stream into the mixture, stirring all the time until ribbons form. Wash and finely chop the onions and sprinkle over the top.

SHELLFISH AND CUCUMBER SALAD

IMPERIAL/METRIC	AMERICAN
¾ lb./375 g. mixed shellfish (prawns, crab, lobster, scallops etc.)	¾ lb. mixed shellfish (shrimp, crab, lobster, scallops etc.)
1 cucumber	1 cucumber
1 teaspoon very finely chopped fresh ginger	1 teaspoon very finely chopped fresh ginger
1 tablespoon soy sauce	1 tablespoon soy sauce
1 tablespoon vinegar	1 tablespoon vinegar
3 tablespoons oil	¼ cup oil
1 teaspoon sugar	1 teaspoon sugar
salt and pepper	salt and pepper
lettuce or Chinese cabbage if available	lettuce or Chinese cabbage if available

METHOD

Cut the shellfish into bite-sized pieces. Peel the cucumber and cut into matchstick strips. Mix together the ginger, soy sauce, vinegar, oil and sugar. Add the shellfish and toss them all together.

Arrange a bed of lettuce leaves in a serving bowl. Put the cucumber on top in a ring and place the shellfish inside the ring of cucumber. Chill.

SHELLFISH FRITTERS

IMPERIAL/METRIC	AMERICAN
1 lb./½ kg. mixed prepared shellfish (prawns, crab, lobster, scallops)	1 lb. mixed prepared shellfish (shrimp, crab, lobster, scallops)
1 clove garlic, crushed	1 clove garlic, crushed
salt and pepper	salt and pepper
3 eggs	3 eggs
2 oz./60 g. plain flour	½ cup all-purpose flour
3 dried mushrooms	3 dried mushrooms
2½ oz./75 g. bamboo shoots	2½ oz. bamboo shoots
8 water chestnuts	8 water chestnuts
1 teaspoon very finely chopped fresh ginger	1 teaspoon very finely chopped fresh ginger
2 sticks celery	2 sticks celery
½ tablespoon soy sauce	½ tablespoon soy sauce
½ tablespoon dry sherry	½ tablespoon dry sherry
¼ pint/1 dcl. chicken stock	¾ cup chicken stock
½ tablespoon cornflour	½ tablespoon cornstarch
pinch of sugar	pinch of sugar
oil for deep frying	oil for deep frying

METHOD

Chop the shellfish and mix with garlic, salt and pepper. Beat the eggs and then beat in the flour and shellfish mixture. Mix together thoroughly.

Soak the mushrooms in warm water for 20 minutes, rinse, squeeze dry and slice, discarding the stalks. Cut the bamboo shoots into matchstick strips and slice the water chestnuts. Cut the celery in diagonal slices.

Mix together in a small saucepan the ginger, soy sauce, sherry, stock, cornflour (cornstarch) and sugar. Bring to the boil, stirring. Add the vegetables and simmer for 2–3 minutes. Heat the oil and drop in teaspoons of the shellfish mixture. Deep fry until golden and crisp. Drain well on absorbent kitchen paper. Serve with sauce poured over.

FRIED LOBSTER WITH CABBAGE

IMPERIAL/METRIC
1 small white cabbage
2 tablespoons oil
½ teaspoon salt
1 lb./½ kg. lobster
   meat
1 tablespoon soy sauce
1 teaspoon brown sugar
1 tablespoon sherry
2 teaspoons cornflour
6 tablespoons water

AMERICAN
1 small white cabbage
2 tablespoons oil
½ tablespoon salt
1 lb. lobster meat

1 tablespoon soy sauce
1 teaspoon brown sugar
1 tablespoon sherry
2 teaspoons cornstarch
½ cup water

METHOD
Wash and drain the cabbage. Shred finely and fry in half the oil for 1 minute over fierce heat, stirring all the time. Add ½ teaspoon salt and 2 tablespoons water, cover and simmer for 2–3 minutes.

Cut the lobster into 1 inch pieces. Fry in the remaining oil for 2–3 minutes. Add the soy sauce, sugar and sherry, stir well. Mix the cornflour (cornstarch) to a smooth paste with the water and add to the pan with the cabbage and its liquid, stirring until slightly thickened.

58

Lobster with bean sprouts

LOBSTER WITH BEAN SPROUTS

IMPERIAL/METRIC	AMERICAN
½ lb./250 g. lobster meat	½ lb. lobster meat
pinch of salt	pinch of salt
pinch of black pepper	pinch of black pepper
1 tablespoon oil	1 tablespoon oil
1 lb./½ kg. bean sprouts	1 lb. bean sprouts
1 teaspoon cornflour	1 teaspoon cornstarch
1 teaspoon brown sugar	1 teaspoon brown sugar
3 tablespoons water	¼ cup water
1 tablespoon soy sauce	1 tablespoon soy sauce
1 spring onion	1 scallion

METHOD

Cut the lobster into neat slices and season with salt and pepper. Heat the oil and fry the lobster for 1 minute. Wash and drain the bean sprouts, then add to the pan, stirring for 1 minute over fierce heat.

Mix the cornflour (cornstarch) and sugar together to a smooth paste with the water and soy sauce. Add to the pan and heat gently, stirring until slightly thickened. Chop the spring onion (scallion) finely, add to the p... mix well.

POULTRY

Chicken is popular in Chinese cookery because, like pork, it is a versatile meat which can be cooked in numerous ways and with a variety of flavourings. As with meat, it is cubed, shredded or sliced; it is also cooked whole and in joints.

For dishes which are cooked quickly, it is advisable to use a young bird, but if the chicken is to be boiled before being incorporated in a dish, a boiling fowl may be used.

Duck, because it has a stronger flavour, offers fewer combinations than chicken and is usually slow-cooked. When it is stir-fried, it is sliced or shredded rather than cubed.

CHICKEN WITH CELERY AND PINEAPPLE SAUCE

IMPERIAL/METRIC	AMERICAN
1 × 2½ lb./1¼ kg. chicken	1 × 2½ lb. chicken
2 sticks celery	2 sticks celery
3 pineapple rings	3 pineapple rings
1 tablespoon cornflour	1 tablespoon cornstarch
1 tablespoon soy sauce	1 tablespoon soy sauce
½ teaspoon very finely chopped fresh ginger	½ teaspoon very finely chopped fresh ginger
4 tablespoons syrup from canned pineapple	⅓ cup syrup from canned pineapple
4 tablespoons brown sugar	⅓ cup brown sugar
4 tablespoons vinegar	⅓ cup vinegar
salt and pepper	salt and pepper
1 egg	1 egg
extra cornflour	extra cornstarch
oil for deep frying	oil for deep frying

METHOD

Place the chicken in a large saucepan and cover with water. Bring to the boil then simmer until tender. (This will be about 1 hour for a young bird or 2–3 hours for a boiling fowl.) Drain and allow to cool.

Cut the celery into diagonal slices and pineapple rings into wedges. In a saucepan, mix together the cornflour (cornstarch), soy sauce and ginger with 4 tablespoons water, pineapple syrup and sugar. Bring to the boil, stirring constantly, stir in the vinegar and cook for 2 minutes. Remove from the heat and add celery and pineapple wedges. Season to taste.

Disjoint the cooled chicken and cut each joint in half to make 8 pieces. Beat the egg with the salt and pepper. Dip the chicken pieces in egg and then in cornflour (cornstarch). Deep fry the chicken in hot oil until golden.

Arrange the chicken on a serving dish. Reheat the sauce and pour it over the chicken pieces.

PAPER (PARCHMENT) WRAPPED CHICKEN

IMPERIAL/METRIC	AMERICAN
2 spring onions	2 scallions
1 oz./30 g. fresh ginger	1 oz. fresh ginger
2 tablespoons soy sauce	2 tablespoons soy sauce
1 tablespoon sherry	1 tablespoon sherry
pinch of brown sugar	pinch of brown sugar
pinch of salt	pinch of salt
pinch of black pepper	pinch of black pepper
1 lb./½ kg. chicken meat	1 lb. chicken meat
deep fat for frying	deep fat for frying

METHOD

Chop the spring onions (scallions) very finely; chop the ginger and mix with the spring onions (scallions), soy sauce, sherry, sugar, salt and pepper. Cut the chicken meat into about 16 slices and toss in the soy sauce mixture. Leave covered for 30 minutes.

Cut out 16 squares of cellophane paper (parchment). Do not use polythene wrapping as this will melt on contact with hot fat. Wrap each piece of chicken in a piece of cellophane (parchment) and secure. Drop the parcels in hot fat and fry for about 3 minutes. Drain.

NOTE: The correct way to serve the chicken is in its wrapper, since the wrapping holds in the flavour and juices.

FRIED CHICKEN SLICES WITH MUSHROOMS

IMPERIAL/METRIC	AMERICAN
1 lb./½ kg. chicken meat	1 lb. chicken meat
1 tablespoon sherry	1 tablespoon sherry
1 teaspoon salt	1 teaspoon salt
1 tablespoon soy sauce	1 tablespoon soy sauce
1 oz./30 g. fresh ginger	1 oz. fresh ginger
1 spring onion	1 scallion
1 tablespoon cornflour	1 tablespoon cornstarch
2 tablespoons water	2 tablespoons water
½ lb./250 g. fresh mushrooms	½ lb. fresh mushrooms
4 tablespoons oil	⅓ cup oil

METHOD

Cut the chicken into paper thin slices and put in a bowl. Mix the sherry, salt and soy sauce together and add to the chicken. Chop the ginger and spring onion (scallion) finely and add to the chicken.

Mix the cornflour (cornstarch) to a smooth paste with the water, add to the chicken. Mix well and leave in a cool place for 30 minutes.

Wash and dry the mushrooms, cut into thin slices. Fry the mushrooms in 1 tablespoon oil for 2 minutes, stirring all the time. Remove and keep hot. Add the remaining oil to the pan, heat and add the chicken; fry over a fierce heat for 1 minute, stirring all the time. Add mushrooms and cook over gentle heat for 3 minutes.

Sweet chicken wings with oyster sauce

SWEET CHICKEN WINGS WITH OYSTER SAUCE

IMPERIAL/METRIC
1 lb./½ kg. chicken wings
3 tablespoons oyster sauce
1 tablespoon soy sauce
½ pint/¼ litre chicken stock
pinch of salt
1 teaspoon brown sugar
1 oz./30 g. fresh ginger
pinch of black pepper
1 teaspoon coarse salt

AMERICAN
1 lb. chicken wings
¼ cup oyster sauce
1 tablespoon soy sauce
1¼ cups chicken stock
pinch of salt
1 teaspoon brown sugar
1 oz. fresh ginger
pinch of black pepper
1 teaspoon coarse salt

METHOD
Wash and dry the chicken wings. Put in a pan with enough cold water to cover, bring to the boil, cover and simmer for 10 minutes. Drain.

Put the chicken wings back into a clean pan, add the oyster sauce, soy sauce, chicken stock, salt and sugar. Bring gently to the boil and simmer for 20 minutes.

Chop the ginger very finely; add the salt and pepper. Sprinkle over the chicken and serve.

Sweet and sour chicken drumsticks

SWEET AND SOUR CHICKEN DRUMSTICKS

IMPERIAL/METRIC	AMERICAN
6 chicken drumsticks	6 chicken drumsticks
1 egg	1 egg
4 tablespoons cornflour	⅓ cup cornstarch
salt and pepper	salt and pepper
1 onion	1 onion
1 small pepper	1 small pepper
1 carrot	1 carrot
¾ pint/3¼ dcl. chicken stock	2 cups chicken stock
4 tablespoons vinegar	⅓ cup vinegar
4 tablespoons soft brown sugar	⅓ cup soft brown sugar
1 tablespoon cornflour	1 tablespoon cornstarch
1 tablespoon soy sauce	1 tablespoon soy sauce
1 tablespoon sherry	1 tablespoon sherry
oil for deep frying	oil for deep frying

METHOD

Trim the drumsticks if necessary. Beat the egg with 1 tablespoon of water. Mix the 4 tablespoons cornflour (⅓ cup cornstarch) with salt and pepper. Dip the drumsticks in egg, then in cornflour (cornstarch) and put to one side.

Cut the onion into eighths and the pepper and carrot into wedges. Drop these into a small saucepan of boiling water and cook for 5 minutes. Drain well. Mix together, in a small saucepan, the chicken stock, vinegar, sugar, cornflour (cornstarch), soy sauce and sherry. Bring to the boil, stirring constantly, and simmer for 2–3 minutes.

Heat the oil in a deep frying pan (skillet) and fry the chicken drumsticks until golden and tender. Drain on absorbent kitchen paper. Add the vegetables to the sauce and then add the chicken. Reheat.

HAM AND MUSHROOM STUFFED CHICKEN

IMPERIAL/METRIC	AMERICAN
4 chicken breasts	4 chicken breasts
2 slices ham	2 slices ham
2 oz./60 g. fresh mushrooms	2 oz. fresh mushrooms
¼ pint/1 dcl. chicken stock	⅔ cup chicken stock
1 tablespoon sherry	1 tablespoon sherry
1 teaspoon cornflour	1 teaspoon cornstarch
1 tablespoon soy sauce	1 tablespoon soy sauce
1 teaspoon sesame oil	1 teaspoon sesame oil

METHOD

Separate the two muscles forming each chicken breast to make 8 pieces. Make a split in each one to form a pocket. Mince (grind) the ham and mushrooms together, divide between the pockets and press the edges together. Lay the pieces in a shallow, greased dish. Add the stock and sherry. Steam for 30 minutes. Lift the chicken on to a hot dish and keep hot.

Mix the cornflour (cornstarch) to a smooth paste with the soy sauce. Add the cooking liquid to the soy mixture, bring to the boil, stirring until slightly thickened. Cook for 1 minute and pour over the chicken.

SATIN CHICKEN

IMPERIAL/METRIC	AMERICAN
1 × 4 lb./2 kg. chicken	1 × 4 lb. chicken
5 oz./150 g. bamboo shoots	5 oz. bamboo shoots
2 tablespoons soy sauce	2 tablespoons soy sauce
2 cloves star anise	2 cloves star anise
1 tablespoon sherry	1 tablespoon sherry
½ teaspoon salt	½ teaspoon salt
1 teaspoon very finely chopped fresh ginger	1 teaspoon very finely chopped fresh ginger
1 clove garlic, crushed	1 clove garlic, crushed
2 tablespoons peanut oil	2 tablespoons peanut oil
¼ pint/1 dcl. chicken stock	¾ cup chicken stock
1 tablespoon cornflour	1 tablespoon cornstarch
½ teaspoon sugar	½ teaspoon sugar

METHOD

Joint the chicken. Slice the bamboo shoots thinly. Mix together the soy sauce, star anise, sherry, salt, ginger and garlic. Rub this mixture all over the chicken pieces and marinate for 1–2 hours.

Heat the oil in a saucepan. Add the chicken pieces and brown them well all over. Add the bamboo shoots and stock. Cover and cook for 20–30 minutes or until the chicken is very tender. Remove the chicken from the bones and cut the meat into long shreds. Mix the cornflour (cornstarch) and sugar with 3 tablespoons (¼ cup) water. Add to the saucepan, bring to the boil, stirring, and simmer for 2–3 minutes. Return the chicken to the saucepan and reheat.

CHICKEN LIVERS WITH PRAWNS (SHRIMP) AND BROCCOLI

IMPERIAL/METRIC	AMERICAN	METHOD
½ lb./250 g. chicken livers	½ lb. chicken livers	Wash and dry the chicken livers, slice thinly and toss in the 2 tablespoons cornflour (cornstarch). Heat the oil and fry the livers for 1 minute. Wash and dry the mushrooms, slice thinly, add to the pan and cook for 1 minute. Chop the onion finely and add to the pan with the salt and pepper. Mix well. Cook the broccoli in salted boiling water for 5 minutes. Drain and add to the pan with the prawns (shrimp).
2 tablespoons cornflour	2 tablespoons cornstarch	
2 tablespoons oil	2 tablespoons oil	
3 oz./90 g. fresh mushrooms	3 oz. fresh mushrooms	
1 spring onion	1 scallion	
pinch of salt	pinch of salt	
pinch of pepper	pinch of pepper	
¾ lb./375 g. frozen broccoli	¾ lb. frozen broccoli	Mix 1 teaspoon cornflour (cornstarch) to a smooth paste with the soy sauce and 5 tablespoons water. Add to the pan. Bring to the boil, stirring until slightly thickened. Cook for 3 minutes.
4 oz./125 g. peeled prawns	4 oz. peeled shrimp	
1 teaspoon cornflour	1 teaspoon cornstarch	
1 tablespoon soy sauce	1 tablespoon soy sauce	

CHICKEN BALLS WITH OYSTER SAUCE

IMPERIAL/METRIC	AMERICAN	METHOD
1 lb./½ kg. chicken meat	1 lb. chicken meat	Cut the chicken into neat pieces as near to ball shapes as possible. Chop the spring onions (scallions) finely, then mix with the soy sauce, sherry and salt. Mix the cornflour (cornstarch) to a smooth paste with water, add the spring onion mixture and mix into the chicken. Mix well. Heat the oil and fry the chicken over fierce heat for 1 minute, stirring all the time. Add the oyster sauce, mix well, and fry gently for about 5 minutes.
2 spring onions	2 scallions	
2 tablespoons soy sauce	2 tablespoons soy sauce	
1 tablespoon sherry	1 tablespoon sherry	
pinch of salt	pinch of salt	
1 tablespoon cornflour	1 tablespoon cornstarch	
2 tablespoons water	2 tablespoons water	
2 tablespoons oil	2 tablespoons oil	
3 tablespoons oyster sauce	¼ cup oyster sauce	

CHICKEN SALAD

IMPERIAL/METRIC	AMERICAN	METHOD
1 × 2 lb./1 kg. chicken	1 × 2 lb. chicken	Joint the chicken. Put the sesame seeds in a small pan and heat gently over a low heat, stirring, until they are toasted golden brown. Crush the ginger and mix with soy sauce, garlic, sugar and half the five-spice powder. Pour this over the chicken and leave for 20 minutes, turning once.
1 teaspoon sesame seeds	1 teaspoon sesame seeds	
1 teaspoon very finely chopped fresh ginger	1 teaspoon very finely chopped fresh ginger	
2 tablespoons soy sauce	2 tablespoons soy sauce	
1 clove garlic, crushed	1 clove garlic, crushed	
3 tablespoons sugar	¼ cup sugar	Drain the chicken and fry it in deep hot oil until tender. Drain well on absorbent kitchen paper. Cool, then remove the meat from the bones and cut it into strips. Chill.
½ teaspoon five-spice powder	½ teaspoon five-spice powder	
oil for deep frying	oil for deep frying	
4 spring onions	4 scallions	
1 stick celery	1 stick celery	Cut the spring onions (scallions) into 1 inch lengths, slice the celery and water chestnuts and cut the bamboo shoots into thin matchstick strips. Mix the chicken with the rest of the five-spice powder and the vegetables. Toss all together lightly. Season. Line a mixing bowl with lettuce leaves. Place the chicken salad in the bowl and sprinkle with a little oil and the toasted sesame seeds.
6 water chestnuts	6 water chestnuts	
5 oz./150 g. bamboo shoots	5 oz. bamboo shoots	
salt and pepper	salt and pepper	
6 lettuce leaves	6 lettuce leaves	

Chicken livers with prawns (shrimp) and broccoli

BRAISED CHICKEN WITH PEPPERS

IMPERIAL/METRIC	AMERICAN
3 red peppers	3 red peppers
1 tablespoon oil	1 tablespoon oil
1 teaspoon salt	1 teaspoon salt
1 lb./½ kg. chicken meat	1 lb. chicken meat
1 oz./30 g. fresh ginger	1 oz. fresh ginger
2 tablespoons oil	2 tablespoons oil
pinch of brown sugar	pinch of brown sugar
2 teaspoons sherry	2 teaspoons sherry
1 teaspoon cornflour	1 teaspoon cornstarch
2 teaspoons soy sauce	2 teaspoons soy sauce

METHOD

Core the peppers and cut into thin rings. Fry in the oil and salt for 1 minute. Add 2 tablespoons water, bring to the boil, cover and simmer for 2 minutes. Drain.

Cut the chicken into 1 inch pieces. Chop the ginger finely, fry both chicken and ginger in oil for 1 minute. Add the sugar and sherry.

Mix the cornflour (cornstarch) to a smooth paste with the soy sauce and add to the pan. Heat gently, stirring until slightly thickened. Add the peppers and cook for 1 minute.

CHICKEN DICE WITH FRIED WALNUTS

IMPERIAL/METRIC	AMERICAN
4 dried mushrooms	4 dried mushrooms
4 oz./125 g. shelled walnuts	4 oz. shelled walnuts
4 tablespoons oil	⅓ cup oil
3 lb./1½ kg. chicken	3 lb. chicken
1 teaspoon cornflour	1 teaspoon cornstarch
1 tablespoon sherry	1 tablespoon sherry
2 tablespoons soy sauce	2 tablespoons soy sauce
1 teaspoon salt	1 teaspoon salt
1 teaspoon brown sugar	1 teaspoon brown sugar

METHOD

Soak the mushrooms in hot water for 10 minutes. Chop the walnuts and fry in 2 tablespoons of the oil for 2 minutes; drain on absorbent kitchen paper to remove all traces of oil.

Cut the chicken meat into small pieces, fry in remaining oil for 3 minutes over fierce heat, stirring all the time. Mix the cornflour (cornstarch) to a smooth paste with the sherry, soy sauce, salt and sugar. Add to the chicken and mix well.

Drain the mushrooms and chop roughly, add to the pan and cook for 2 minutes. Add the walnuts.

CHICKEN WINGS WITH MUSHROOMS

IMPERIAL/METRIC	AMERICAN
2 tablespoons soy sauce	2 tablespoons soy sauce
1 teaspoon salt	1 teaspoon salt
12 chicken wings	12 chicken wings
1 teaspoon finely chopped fresh ginger	1 teaspoon finely chopped fresh ginger
6 dried mushrooms	6 dried mushrooms
4 tablespoons peanut oil	⅓ cup peanut oil
½ lb./250 g. snow peas	½ lb. snow peas
2 spring onions, sliced	2 scallions, sliced
1 tablespoon sherry	1 tablespoon sherry
pinch of sugar	pinch of sugar
pinch of monosodium glutamate	pinch of monosodium glutamate
¼ pint/1 dcl. chicken stock	¾ cup chicken stock
1 tablespoon cornflour	1 tablespoon cornstarch

METHOD

Sprinkle soy sauce and salt over chicken wings and marinate for 30 minutes, turning occasionally.

Soak the mushrooms in warm water for 20 minutes, rinse, squeeze dry and cut into thin strips; discard the stalks. String the snow peas and cook, in their pods, in ½ inch of boiling salted water for 5 minutes.

Heat the oil and fry the chicken until golden brown and tender. Pour off excess oil. Add the mushrooms, marinade, spring onions (scallions), sherry, sugar, monosodium glutamate and the chicken stock. Bring to the boil and simmer for 3 minutes. Mix the cornflour (cornstarch) with a little water and add to the pan. Simmer, stirring, for 2 minutes. Add the snow peas and cook for 1 minute.

NOTE: Snow peas are available from some greengrocers or they can be bought from Chinese food stores. They are sometimes called 'mange-tout' as the pods are eaten as well as the peas. If you cannot buy snow peas, broccoli may be used.

Braised chicken with peppers

BRAISED CHICKEN WITH VEGETABLES

IMPERIAL/METRIC	AMERICAN
1 × 2½ lb./1¼ kg. chicken	1 × 2½ lb. chicken
3 tablespoons soy sauce	¼ cup soy sauce
1 tablespoon dry sherry (optional)	1 tablespoon dry sherry (optional)
½ teaspoon sugar	½ teaspoon sugar
1 teaspoon salt	1 teaspoon salt
1 pineapple ring	1 pineapple ring
1 small pepper	1 small pepper
1 carrot	1 carrot
1 stick celery	1 stick celery
3 water chestnuts	3 water chestnuts
2 tablespoons peanut oil	2 tablespoons peanut oil
2 cloves garlic, crushed	2 cloves garlic, crushed
1 teaspoon very finely chopped fresh ginger	1 teaspoon very finely chopped fresh ginger
¾ pint/3½ dcl. chicken stock	2 cups chicken stock
1 spring onion, sliced	1 scallion, sliced
4 oz./125 g. spinach, finely shredded	4 oz. spinach, finely shredded
1 tablespoon brown sugar	1 tablespoon brown sugar
1½ tablespoons cornflour	1½ tablespoons cornstarch

METHOD

Joint the chicken and cut each joint in half to make 8 pieces. Mix together the soy sauce, sherry, sugar and salt. Rub this all over the chicken pieces and leave for at least 20 minutes. Cut the pineapple into eighths and the pepper and carrot into wedges. Drop these into a small saucepan of boiling water, cook for 5 minutes, and drain. Cut the celery diagonally and slice the water chestnuts into thin rounds.

Heat the oil in a frying pan (skillet) and add the garlic and ginger. Fry, stirring, for 2 minutes. Add the chicken pieces and brown them all over. Pour off excess oil, add the chicken stock, bring to the boil and simmer, covered for 30 minutes. Add the pineapple and vegetables to the pan and continue cooking until the chicken is very tender.

Arrange the chicken on a hot serving dish. Mix the sugar and cornflour (cornstarch) with a little water and add to the cooking liquid. Bring to the boil, stirring constantly, and cook for 2–3 minutes. Adjust the seasoning. Serve with the sauce poured over the chicken.

NOTE: A little finely minced (ground) barbecued pork is delicious added to this dish.

CRISP SKIN CHICKEN

IMPERIAL/METRIC	AMERICAN
1 × 2½ lb./1¼ kg. chicken	1 × 2½ lb. chicken
1 tablespoon vinegar	1 tablespoon vinegar
2 tablespoons soy sauce	2 tablespoons soy sauce
2 tablespoons honey	2 tablespoons honey
1 tablespoon sherry	1 tablespoon sherry
1 teaspoon treacle	1 teaspoon molasses
2 tablespoons plain flour	2 tablespoons all-purpose flour
1 teaspoon salt	1 teaspoon salt
peanut oil for deep frying	peanut oil for deep frying

METHOD

Put the chicken in a large saucepan and add boiling water to come halfway up the sides of the chicken. Cover tightly and simmer until just tender, about 45 minutes to 1 hour. Drain, rinse under cold water and dry with kitchen paper.

Mix together the vinegar, soy sauce, honey, sherry and treacle (molasses). Brush this all over the chicken and then hang the chicken in an airy place to dry, for about 30 minutes. Brush over the remaining soy sauce mixture and hang again for 20–30 minutes. Mix the flour and salt together and rub well into the chicken skin. Fry in deep hot peanut oil until golden and crisp. Drain well on absorbent kitchen paper.

Chop the chicken into 8 pieces and serve warm with the following dips.

Cinnamon Dip: Mix together 1 tablespoon ground cinnamon, ½ teaspoon ground ginger, ¼ teaspoon each freshly ground black pepper and salt. Place in a small saucepan and heat until very hot, stirring constantly.

Pepper and Salt Dip: Mix together 1 tablespoon salt and ½ tablespoon freshly ground black pepper. Place in a small saucepan and heat, stirring, until the salt begins to brown.

Hoi Sin Sauce

Guests dip the pieces of chicken into the dips, which are served separately in small bowls.

NOTE: As this dish is eaten with the fingers, place finger bowls of cold water on the table.

RED COOKED CHICKEN WITH CHESTNUTS

IMPERIAL/METRIC	AMERICAN
1 lb./½ kg. dried chestnuts	1 lb. dried chestnuts
5 lb./2½ kg. chicken	5 lb. chicken
3 tablespoons oil	¼ cup oil
1 pint/½ litre water	2½ cups water
4 tablespoons soy sauce	⅓ cup soy sauce
2 tablespoons sherry	2 tablespoons sherry
1 oz./30 g. fresh ginger	1 oz. fresh ginger
1 spring onion	1 scallion
1 teaspoon brown sugar	1 teaspoon brown sugar

METHOD

Cook the chestnuts in 2 pints (1 litre/5 cups) boiling water for about 2 hours. Remove the brown skins and leave the nuts in the water.

Meanwhile cut the chicken into neat small pieces. Fry them in hot oil for about 5 minutes, or until lightly browned all over. Add the remaining ingredients with the exception of the brown sugar and cover the pan tightly. Simmer for 30 minutes. Add the chestnuts and half the liquid with the brown sugar. Bring to the boil, cover and simmer for 10 minutes.

Chicken chop suey on boiled rice; Pork with chicken and vegetables (page 24)

CHICKEN CHOP SUEY

IMPERIAL/METRIC	AMERICAN
4 dried mushrooms	4 dried mushrooms
5 oz./150 g. canned bamboo shoots	5 oz. canned bamboo shoots
1 onion	1 onion
1 pepper	1 pepper
1 lb./½ kg. canned bean sprouts	1 lb. canned bean sprouts
¾ lb./375 g. cooked chicken	3 cups cooked chicken
2 tablespoons peanut oil	2 tablespoons peanut oil
½ pint/¼ litre chicken stock	1¼ cups chicken stock
½ teaspoon sugar	½ teaspoon sugar
1 teaspoon soy sauce	1 teaspoon soy sauce
salt and pepper to taste	salt and pepper to taste
1 teaspoon cornflour	1 teaspoon cornstarch
1 tablespoon dry sherry	1 tablespoon dry sherry

METHOD

Soak the mushrooms in warm water for 20 minutes, rinse, squeeze dry and cut into thin slices, discarding the stalks. Cut the bamboo shoot into thin strips. Cut the onion into eighths. Slice pepper thinly. Drain the bean sprouts, rinse in cold running water and drain again. Cut the chicken into ½ inch cubes.

Heat the oil in a saucepan and add the chicken and vegetables. Cook, stirring, for 3–4 minutes. Add the stock, sugar, soy sauce and seasonings, bring to the boil, stirring constantly, and simmer for 5 minutes. Mix the cornflour (cornstarch) with sherry and add to the saucepan. Bring to the boil, stirring constantly, and cook for a further 3 minutes.

DUCK WITH ALMONDS

IMPERIAL/METRIC	AMERICAN
1 lb./½ kg. duck meat	1 lb. duck meat
2 tablespoons oil	2 tablespoons oil
1 teaspoon salt	1 teaspoon salt
2 tablespoons soy sauce	2 tablespoons soy sauce
2 sticks celery	2 sticks celery
2 oz./60 g. fresh mushrooms	2 oz. fresh mushrooms
4 oz./125 g. frozen peas	4 oz. frozen peas
½ pint/¼ litre stock	1¼ cups stock
2 teaspoons cornflour	2 teaspoons cornstarch
3 oz./90 g. split, browned almonds	3 oz. split, toasted almonds

METHOD

Cut the duck meat into paper thin slices. Heat the oil, add the salt and duck and fry for about 5 minutes or until the meat is tender. Add the soy sauce and mix well.

Wash and chop the celery; wash and thinly slice the mushrooms; add both to the pan with the peas, mix well and cook for 1 minute. Add the stock, bring to the boil and simmer for 5 minutes.

Mix the cornflour (cornstarch) to a smooth paste with a little cold water, stir into the pan, bring to the boil, stirring all the time until slightly thickened.

Add the almonds and serve.

ONION DUCK

IMPERIAL/METRIC	AMERICAN
1 × 4 lb./2 kg. duck	1 × 4 lb. duck
1 lb./½ kg. onions	1 lb. onions
6 tablespoons soy sauce	½ cup soy sauce
2 tablespoons oil	2 tablespoons oil
1 tablespoon brown sugar	1 tablespoon brown sugar
2 tablespoons sherry	2 tablespoons sherry

METHOD

Wash and dry the duck. Peel and thickly slice the onions, mix with 2 tablespoons of the soy sauce and push inside the duck.

Heat the oil and fry the duck gently for 10 minutes to brown slightly all over. Drain and place in a large pot. Add 2 pints (1 litre/5 cups) water, the remaining soy sauce, sugar and the sherry. Bring to the boil, cover and simmer for 1 hour, turn the duck over and simmer for another 30 minutes.

NOTE: The liquid in the pot can be thickened, with 2 teaspoons cornflour (cornstarch) mixed to a smooth paste with a little water, and poured over the duck as a sauce.

Duck with almonds

CRISP DUCK WITH FIVE SPICES

IMPERIAL/METRIC	AMERICAN
1 × 4 lb./2 kg. duck	1 × 4 lb. duck
2 tablespoons soy sauce	2 tablespoons soy sauce
2 cloves star anise	2 cloves star anise
1 teaspoon salt	1 teaspoon salt
1 tablespoon brown sugar	1 tablespoon brown sugar
2 teaspoons five-spice powder	2 teaspoons five-spice powder
1 tablespoon salted black beans	1 tablespoon salted black beans
1 tablespoon sherry	1 tablespoon sherry
1 tablespoon cornflour	1 tablespoon cornstarch
1 tablespoon plain flour	1 tablespoon all-purpose flour
peanut oil for deep frying	peanut oil for deep frying
fruit chutney for serving	fruit chutney for serving

METHOD

Place the duck in a large saucepan and add 1½ pints (¾ litre/3¾ cups) water, the soy sauce, star anise, salt, and brown sugar. Bring to the boil and simmer until tender, about 2 hours. Drain the duck well and dry with absorbent kitchen paper. Mix the five-spice powder with the beans and sherry and mash very thoroughly. Place 1 teaspoon of the mixture inside the duck and rub the rest over the outside. Sift the flours together and pat on to the outside of the duck. Deep fry the duck in hot oil until golden and crisp. Drain well on kitchen paper.

Chop into eighths through the bones and serve warm with a fruit chutney.

NOTE: Supply finger bowls as this dish is eaten with the fingers.

WEST LAKE STEAMED DUCK

IMPERIAL/METRIC	AMERICAN
1 lb./½ kg. white cabbage	1 lb. white cabbage
6 oz./180 g. ham	6 oz. ham
1 teaspoon salt	1 teaspoon salt
1 tablespoon lotus seeds	1 tablespoon lotus seeds
1 × 5 lb./2½ kg. duck	1 × 5 lb. duck
4 tablespoons oil	⅓ cup oil

METHOD

Shred the cabbage, wash and drain. Chop the ham; add one third of the cabbage with the salt and lotus seeds.

Wash and dry the duck, then stuff with the cabbage mixture, secure the opening and fry gently in the oil for about 20 minutes, turning often to brown all over.

Put the rest of the cabbage in a bowl, place the duck on top and cover with foil. Stand the bowl in a large saucepan, half fill with water and simmer for about 3 hours or until the duck is tender.

Serve the duck on the cabbage.

BRAISED DUCK WITH SWEET AND PUNGENT SAUCE

IMPERIAL/METRIC

1 × 4 lb./2 kg. duck
salt
1 clove garlic, crushed
3 spring onions, very
    finely chopped
3 tablespoons soy sauce
2 tablespoons sherry
2 tablespoons honey
Sauce:
1 small green pepper
5 oz./150 g. canned
    bamboo shoots
2 dried mushrooms
1 teaspoon finely chopped
    fresh ginger
1 clove garlic, crushed
2 tablespoons oil
¼ pint/1 dcl. pineapple
    juice
2 tablespoons vinegar
1 teaspoon tomato paste
1 tablespoon dry sherry
1 tablespoon soy sauce
salt and pepper
2 tablespoons cornflour
11 oz./340 g. canned
    mandarin oranges
4 pineapple rings,
    chopped

AMERICAN

1 × 4 lb. duck
salt
1 clove garlic, crushed
3 scallions, very finely
    chopped
¼ cup soy sauce
2 tablespoons sherry
2 tablespoons honey
Sauce:
1 small green pepper
5 oz. canned bamboo
    shoots
2 dried mushrooms
1 teaspoon finely chopped
    fresh ginger
1 clove garlic, crushed
2 tablespoons oil
¾ cup pineapple juice

2 tablespoons vinegar
1 teaspoon tomato paste
1 tablespoon dry sherry
1 tablespoon soy sauce
salt and pepper
2 tablespoons cornstarch
11 oz. canned mandarin
    oranges
4 pineapple rings,
    chopped

METHOD

Wipe the duck inside and out with a damp cloth and rub it all over with salt. Mix the garlic, spring onions (scallions), soy sauce and sherry together. Divide the mixture into two and mix honey into one half. Rub the outside of the duck with some of the honey mixture and allow to dry.

Place the duck on a rack in a roasting pan and pour the soy sauce (*not* the honey) mixture inside. Pour 2 inches of water into a roasting pan and cook the duck in a moderate oven (350°F/180°C, Mark 4) for 1¾–2 hours or until tender, with the flesh coming away from the bones easily. Add ½ pint (¼ litre/1¼ cups) of boiling water to the remaining honey mixture and baste with this every 20 minutes.

Sauce: Cut the pepper into wedges and the bamboo shoot into thin strips. Soak the mushrooms in warm water for 20 minutes, rinse, squeeze dry and slice, discarding the stalks. Place the oil in a saucepan and fry the prepared vegetables with the ginger and garlic for 5 minutes. Add the stock and bring to the boil. Add the honey, pineapple juice and vinegar, bring to the boil again and stir until the honey has melted. Stir in the tomato paste, sherry, soy sauce and salt and pepper to taste. Mix the cornflour (cornstarch) with a little water and add to the pan. Bring to the boil, stirring constantly and simmer for 2–3 minutes.

Garnish the duck with the mandarin orange segments and pineapple wedges. Pour the sauce over the duck and serve hot.

NOTE: Make the stock from the duck giblets or use a chicken stock cube.

DUCK WITH BLACK BEANS

IMPERIAL/METRIC

2 teaspoons cornflour
2 teaspoons soy sauce
1 teaspoon sesame oil
pinch of salt
pinch of black pepper
6 oz./180 g. cooked
    duck meat
1 oz./30 g. fresh ginger
3 oz./90 g. black beans
1 clove garlic
1 spring onion
2 tablespoons oil or
    melted lard
¼ pint/1 dcl. chicken
    stock
1 tablespoon sherry

AMERICAN

2 teaspoons cornstarch
2 teaspoons soy sauce
1 teaspoon sesame oil
pinch of salt
pinch of black pepper
6 oz. cooked duck meat

1 oz. fresh ginger
3 oz. black beans
1 clove garlic
1 scallion
2 tablespoons oil or
    melted lard
¾ cup chicken stock

1 tablespoon sherry

METHOD

Mix the cornflour (cornstarch) to a smooth paste with the soy sauce, sesame oil, salt and pepper. Cut the duck meat into small dice, add to the soy mixture, mix well and leave, covered, for 10 minutes.

Chop the ginger very finely; mash the beans with a fork; crush the garlic; chop the onion finely; mix well together and pound into a paste.

Heat the oil or lard and fry the duck for 3 minutes. Add the paste and fry for 1 minute. Add the stock and sherry, mix well and simmer for 2 minutes.

DUCK WITH PRAWN (SHRIMP) SAUCE

IMPERIAL/METRIC
½ lb./250 g. duck meat
1 tablespoon sherry
pinch of salt
pinch of black pepper
½ teaspoon ground ginger
1 clove garlic
1 egg
2 tablespoons cornflour
deep fat for frying
4 oz./125 g. prawns
1 teaspoon soy sauce
½ pint/¼ litre chicken
   stock
2 spring onions

AMERICAN
½ lb. duck meat
1 tablespoon sherry
pinch of salt
pinch of black pepper
½ teaspoon ground ginger
1 clove garlic
1 egg
2 tablespoons cornstarch
deep fat for frying
4 oz. shrimp
1 teaspoon soy sauce
1¼ cups chicken stock
2 scallions

METHOD
Cut the duck meat into paper thin slices. Mix the sherry, salt and pepper, ginger and crushed garlic together in a shallow dish. Add the duck, toss well in the mixture and leave for 5 minutes. Beat the egg, add to the duck and mix well until the duck is completely coated with egg. Add half the cornflour (cornstarch) and mix well. Heat the fat and fry the duck pieces for 3 minutes. Drain and keep hot.

Chop the prawns (shrimp) finely, add the soy sauce and put in a clean pan with the stock, heat gently.

Mix the remaining cornflour (cornstarch) to a smooth paste with a little cold water, add to the pan and bring to the boil, stirring all the time until thickened. Pile the duck on a large dish and pour the sauce over. Finely chop the spring onions (scallions) and sprinkle over the duck.

Braised duck with sweet and pungent sauce

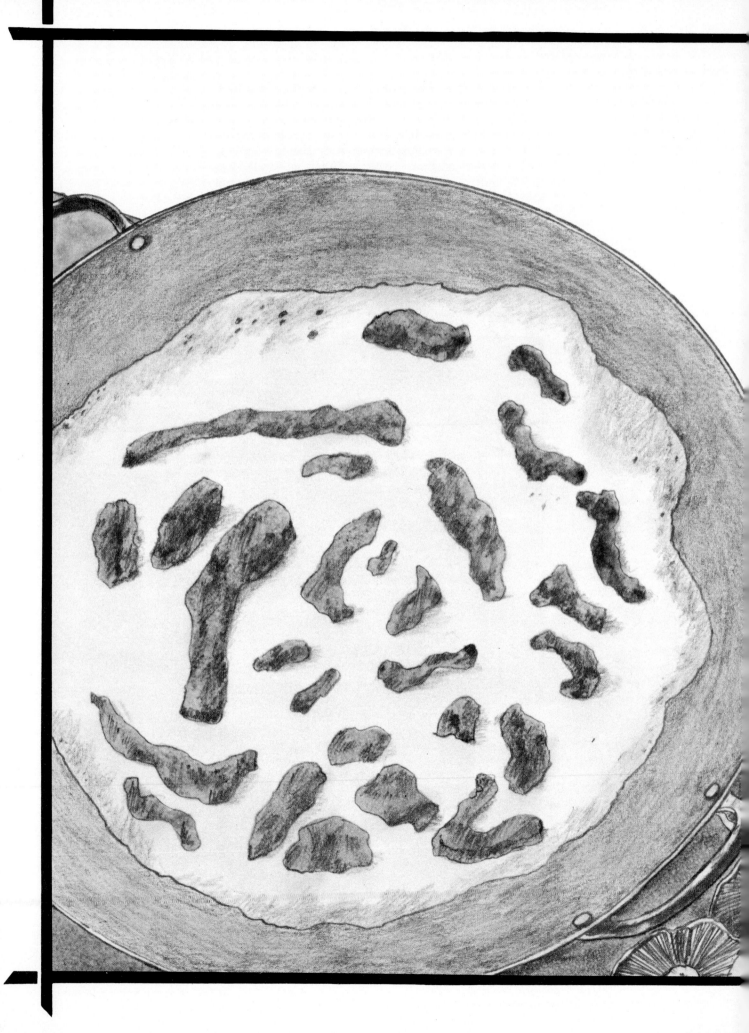

EGGS

In Chinese cookery eggs are used more as an ingredient in combination with other foods rather than as a dish on their own; beaten egg is often stirred into soups, or used as a garnish for dishes in the form of omelet strips. There are, however, several recipes using eggs as a main ingredient and they are useful for serving as light meals or snacks. It is important to serve egg dishes as soon as they are cooked as they become unappetizing if kept waiting.

Probably the most famous of Chinese egg dishes is the 100-year eggs, which are eggs preserved in lime. They are not, however, 100 years old as the name suggests – they merely look that age. These eggs are considered to be at their best at $3\frac{1}{2}$ months – that is, 100 days.

SCRAMBLED EGGS WITH PRAWNS (SHRIMP)

IMPERIAL/METRIC	AMERICAN
6 oz./180 g. peeled prawns	6 oz. peeled shrimp
1 spring onion	1 scallion
1 oz./30 g. fresh mushrooms	1 oz. fresh mushrooms
1 oz./30 g. lard or dripping	1 oz. lard or dripping
6 eggs	6 eggs
3 tablespoons sherry	¼ cup sherry
1 teaspoon salt	1 teaspoon salt
pinch of black pepper	pinch of black pepper

METHOD

Chop the prawns (shrimp) roughly; wash and chop the spring onion (scallion); wash and slice the mushrooms. Melt the fat and fry the prawns (shrimp), onion and mushrooms for 1 minute.

Beat the eggs, sherry, salt and pepper together until smooth. Pour on to the ingredients in the pan and stir briskly for 1–2 minutes until scrambled and set.

STEAMED EGGS WITH CRAB

IMPERIAL/METRIC	AMERICAN
6 eggs	6 eggs
¾ pint/3½ dcl. chicken stock	2 cups chicken stock
1 teaspoon dry sherry	1 teaspoon dry sherry
1 tablespoon soy sauce	1 tablespoon soy sauce
½ tablespoon peanut oil	½ tablespoon peanut oil
4 oz./125 g. chopped crab	1 cup chopped crab
salt and pepper	salt and pepper

METHOD

Beat the eggs and add all the other ingredients. Pour into an oiled pudding basin and cover with greaseproof (waxed) paper and then a layer of aluminium foil. Tie down securely. Place in a steamer over gently simmering water for 30–40 minutes or until set (when cooked, the tip of a knife inserted in the eggs will come out clean).
NOTE: Try using other seafood in this recipe, such as prawns (shrimp) or scallops, instead of crab meat.

LIANG-FAR EGGS

IMPERIAL/METRIC	AMERICAN
2 dried mushrooms	2 dried mushrooms
4 oz./125 g. Chinese cabbage or spinach	4 oz. Chinese cabbage or spinach
4 sticks celery	4 sticks celery
5 oz./150 g. bamboo shoots	5 oz. bamboo shoots
2 teaspoons soy sauce	2 teaspoons soy sauce
1 tablespoon dry sherry	1 tablespoon dry sherry
½ teaspoon sugar	½ teaspoon sugar
¼ pint/1 dcl. chicken stock	¾ cup chicken stock
1 tablespoon cornflour	1 tablespoon cornstarch
pinch of monosodium glutamate	pinch of monosodium glutamate
oil for frying	oil for frying
1 clove garlic, crushed	1 clove garlic, crushed
½ teaspoon salt	½ teaspoon salt
6 eggs	6 eggs
lettuce for serving	lettuce for serving

METHOD

Soak the mushrooms in warm water for 20 minutes, rinse, squeeze dry and slice thinly, discarding the stalks. Shred the cabbage finely. Cut the celery diagonally. Cut the bamboo shoots into thin strips. Mix together the soy sauce, sherry, sugar, stock, cornflour (cornstarch) and monosodium glutamate. Heat 1 tablespoon oil in a saucepan with the garlic and salt. Add the prepared vegetables and continue cooking, stirring, for 2–3 minutes. Stir the cornflour (cornstarch) mixture and add to the pan. Bring to the boil, stirring, and simmer for 2–3 minutes. Keep hot.

Heat about one inch of oil in a small frying pan (skillet). Fry the eggs. Arrange the lettuce on a serving dish, put the eggs on top and pour the sauce over.

Liang-far eggs

BRAISED EGGS

IMPERIAL/METRIC	AMERICAN
6 eggs	6 eggs
4 tablespoons soy sauce	⅓ cup soy sauce
2 tablespoons peanut or sunflower oil	2 tablespoons peanut or sunflower oil

METHOD

Cook the eggs in boiling water for 5 minutes, remove from the pan and leave under cold running water for 5 minutes. Remove the shells.

Mix the soy sauce and oil together. Heat gently. Add the eggs and turn in the mixture for 5 minutes or until brown. Leave to cool in the mixture, remove and cut into quarters for serving.

PRAWN (SHRIMP) OMELETS

IMPERIAL/METRIC	AMERICAN
4 eggs	4 eggs
1 spring onion	1 scallion
2 oz./60 g. prawns	½ cup shrimp
salt	salt
pinch of monosodium glutamate	pinch of monosodium glutamate
¼ pint/1 dcl. chicken stock	¾ cup chicken stock
oil for frying	oil for frying
1 tablespoon soy sauce	1 tablespoon soy sauce
1 tablespoon cornflour	1 tablespoon cornstarch
1 teaspoon sugar	1 teaspoon sugar

METHOD

Beat the eggs and chop the spring onion (scallion) finely. Mix the eggs with the prawns (shrimp), onion, pinch of salt, monosodium glutamate and 2 tablespoons of the chicken stock. Heat a little oil in a small pan, add ¼ of the egg mixture and fry until golden underneath, stirring occasionally with a fork. Fold in half and keep warm on a plate. Make 3 more omelets. Place all the remaining ingredients in a saucepan, bring to the boil, stirring constantly, and simmer for 2–3 minutes. Pour the sauce over the omelets and serve immediately.

NOTE: This dish is good served as part of a meal, as an appetizer before the main course or simply as a snack. It can also be made as one large omelet and cut into serving pieces.

Prawn omelet

MIXED OMELET

IMPERIAL/METRIC	AMERICAN	METHOD
3 eggs	3 eggs	Beat the eggs with salt and add the peas. Cut the pepper into matchstick strips and cook in boiling water for 5 minutes. Cut the spring onions (scallions) into thin slices. Add the pepper and spring onions (scallions) to the eggs.
½ teaspoon salt	½ teaspoon salt	
2 tablespoons cooked or frozen peas	2 tablespoons cooked or frozen peas	
1 red pepper	1 red pepper	
2 spring onions	2 scallions	
1 tablespoon peanut oil	1 tablespoon peanut oil	Heat the oil in a frying pan (skillet), add the pork and cook, stirring until the colour changes. Pour the eggs into the pan, cook for 1 minute, and add the sherry, soy sauce and sugar. Continue cooking until the omelet is cooked but still moist on top.
4 oz./125 g. minced lean pork	½ cup ground lean pork	
½ tablespoon dry sherry, optional	½ tablespoon dry sherry, optional	
½ tablespoon soy sauce	½ tablespoon soy sauce	
pinch of sugar	pinch of sugar	

VEGETABLE OMELETS WITH SWEET AND SOUR SAUCE

IMPERIAL/METRIC	AMERICAN	METHOD
4 dried mushrooms	4 dried mushrooms	Soak the mushrooms in warm water for 20 minutes, rinse, squeeze dry and slice thinly, discarding the stalks. Drain the bean sprouts, rinse in cold water and drain again. Slice the celery diagonally and cut the spring onions (scallions) into thin rounds. Cook the mushrooms and celery in boiling water for 3 minutes, strain. Beat the eggs and add the soy sauce, salt and pepper, and prepared vegetables.
1 lb./½ kg. bean sprouts	1 lb. bean sprouts	
3 sticks celery	3 sticks celery	
2 spring onions	2 scallions	
4 eggs	4 eggs	
1 tablespoon soy sauce	1 tablespoon soy sauce	
salt and pepper	salt and pepper	
2 tablespoons vinegar	2 tablespoons vinegar	Mix together in a small saucepan the vinegar, sugar, tomato paste, cornflour (cornstarch) and ginger. Cut the pepper and the pineapple rings into wedges and add them to the saucepan with the pineapple syrup and 2 tablespoons water. Bring to the boil, stirring constantly, and simmer for 3–4 minutes.
1 tablespoon sugar	1 tablespoon sugar	
1 tablespoon tomato paste	1 tablespoon tomato paste	
1 teaspoon cornflour	1 teaspoon cornstarch	
½ teaspoon very finely chopped fresh ginger	½ teaspoon very finely chopped fresh ginger	
1 red pepper	1 red pepper	
2 pineapple rings	2 pineapple rings	Heat enough oil to cover lightly the base of a small omelet pan. Add a generous tablespoon of the egg mixture and cook rapidly until lightly browned underneath. Place on a heated serving dish and keep hot. Continue cooking until all the egg mixture has been made into small omelets. Pour the sauce over.
2 tablespoons syrup from canned pineapple	2 tablespoons syrup from canned pineapple	
oil for frying	oil for frying	

PORK OMELET

IMPERIAL/METRIC	AMERICAN	METHOD
1 lb./½ kg. lean pork	1 lb. lean pork	Cut the pork into paper thin slices and mix with the soy sauce. Heat the fat in a large frying pan (skillet), add the meat and fry over fierce heat for 1 minute, stirring all the time.
2 tablespoons soy sauce	2 tablespoons soy sauce	
1 oz./30 g. lard	1 oz. lard	
6 eggs	6 eggs	Beat the eggs and salt together until smooth. Pour on to the meat and stir well until set.
1 teaspoon salt	1 teaspoon salt	

NOTE: Often a double quantity is made; one half is heated in stock and served as soup.

EGG AND HAM DUMPLINGS

IMPERIAL/METRIC	AMERICAN
1 lb./½ kg. ham	1 lb. ham
4 eggs	4 eggs
2 oz./60 g. white breadcrumbs	2 oz. white breadcrumbs
1 teaspoon plain flour	1 teaspoon all-purpose flour
deep fat for frying	deep fat for frying

METHOD
Mince (grind) the ham, mix with the eggs and bread-crumbs, beating well until smooth. Shape the mixture into small balls. Heat the fat until smoking and fry the dumplings four at a time until golden brown. Drain on kitchen paper and serve.

EGGS WITH CRAB AND BEAN SPROUTS

IMPERIAL/METRIC	AMERICAN
7 oz./200 g. crab meat	7 oz. crab meat
1 oz./30 g. lard	1 oz. lard
½ lb./250 g. bean sprouts	½ lb. bean sprouts
6 eggs	6 eggs
1 teaspoon salt	1 teaspoon salt
pinch of black pepper	pinch of black pepper
2 spring onions	2 scallions

METHOD
Chop the crab meat. Heat the fat and fry the crab, stirring all the time, for 1 minute. Wash and drain the bean sprouts, add to the crab and cook for 2–3 minutes.

Beat the eggs, salt and pepper together until smooth. Pour into the pan and stir gently over low heat until the eggs are set.

Wash and finely chop the spring onions (scallions), sprinkle over the egg mixture and serve.

EGG THREADS

IMPERIAL/METRIC	AMERICAN
2 eggs	2 eggs
2 tablespoons peanut or sunflower oil	2 tablespoons peanut or sunflower oil

METHOD
Beat the eggs until smooth. Heat the oil in a large frying pan (skillet), but not too hot. Pour the eggs in gently, so that they form a thin layer over the base of the pan. Allow to set.

Remove from the pan, cool and cut into very thin strips, about 4 inches long. Use the rest of the eggs in the same way.

NOTE: Use egg threads as a garnish over such dishes as fried noodles, etc.

SWEET AND SOUR EGGS

IMPERIAL/METRIC	AMERICAN
4 water chestnuts	4 water chestnuts
1 carrot	1 carrot
¼ pint/1 dcl. chicken stock	¾ cup chicken stock
1 clove garlic, crushed	1 clove garlic, crushed
1 tablespoon peanut oil	1 tablespoon peanut oil
2 tablespoons sugar	2 tablespoons sugar
2 tablespoons vinegar	2 tablespoons vinegar
1 teaspoon tomato paste	1 teaspoon tomato paste
½ teaspoon salt	½ teaspoon salt
1 tablespoon cornflour	1 tablespoon cornstarch
4 eggs	4 eggs
oil for frying	oil for frying

METHOD
Slice the water chestnuts thinly and the carrot in wedges. Mix together in a small saucepan the stock, garlic, peanut oil, sugar, vinegar, tomato paste, salt, and cornflour (cornstarch). Bring to the boil, stirring constantly, then add the vegetables and simmer for 4–5 minutes.

Beat each egg separately with 1 teaspoon water. Heat a little oil in a small omelet pan and make 4 omelets, one after the other. Fold the omelets and place on a serving dish. Pour the sauce over and serve.

PRESERVED CHINESE EGGS

Chinese preserved eggs are sold in shops which specialize in Chinese foods. They look very unappetizing but can make an unusual addition to a Chinese meal or can be served as an appetizer before the main course.

The grey coating of clay and rice husks is cracked and carefully removed. The eggs are then cut into quarters lengthways and are served with Chinese mixed pickles, soy sauce and finely chopped ginger.

Sweet and sour eggs; preserved Chinese eggs

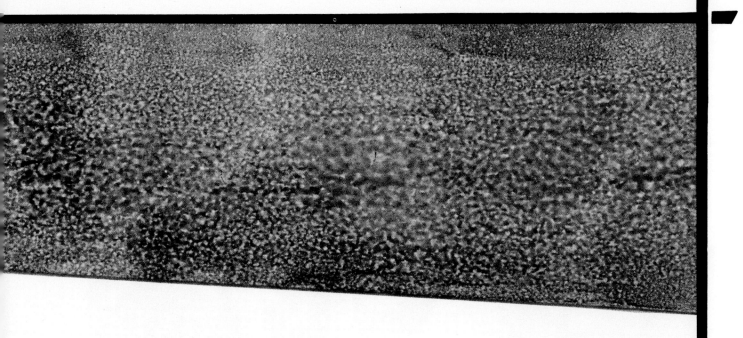

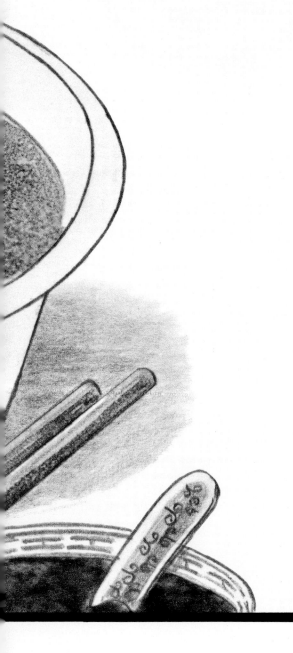

SOUPS

In a Chinese meal soup has quite a different function from its Western counterpart. It is not served merely at the beginning of the meal but is supped between the various courses. As Chinese soup is very light, it serves to refresh the palate and aid the digestion, particularly after very rich dishes.

The basis of Chinese soup is good, clear stock, made from pork, veal, chicken or ham. It is made in the same way as Western stock but the proportion of meat to water is much higher, so it has a more pronounced flavour which is then enhanced by the addition of vegetables, fish, meat or chicken. An even better stock is made from chicken and pork, using $\frac{1}{2}$ lb. (250 g.) of each meat to 1 pint ($\frac{1}{2}$ litre) of water.

Chinese soup should always be served piping hot. Soup containing vegetables should be served as soon as possible after cooking as the vegetables should retain some of their crispness. If egg is to be added to the soup, do this just before serving.

*Chicken, ham and
mushroom soup in preparation*

MIXED VEGETABLE SOUP

IMPERIAL/METRIC	AMERICAN
2 carrots	2 carrots
1 small turnip	1 small turnip
3 oz./90 g. bamboo shoots	3 oz. bamboo shoots
4 oz./125 g. white cabbage	4 oz. white cabbage
3 teaspoons salt	3 teaspoons salt
2 large tomatoes	2 large tomatoes
2 pints/1 litre water	5 cups water
3 oz./90 g. noodles	3 oz. noodles
3 oz./90 g. Chinese pickles (cha tsai)	3 oz. Chinese pickles (cha tsai)
2 spring onions	2 scallions
3 oz./90 g. pea sprouts	3 oz. pea sprouts
2 tablespoons Vesop	2 tablespoons Vesop
½ teaspoon monosodium glutamate	½ teaspoon monosodium glutamate
pinch of pepper	pinch of pepper

METHOD

Peel the carrots and turnip, shred or grate the flesh
finely; grate the bamboo shoots; wash and shred the
cabbage; mix 1 teaspoon of the salt with these vegetables.
Slice the tomatoes. Fry vegetables in a little oil for 5
minutes, stirring well. Add the water, mix well, then stir
in the noodles. Simmer for 30 minutes.

Slice the pickles; chop the spring onions (scallions);
add with pea sprouts to the pan and cook for 5 minutes.
Add remaining ingredients and simmer for 10 minutes.

CHICKEN, HAM AND MUSHROOM SOUP

IMPERIAL/METRIC	AMERICAN
8 dried mushrooms	8 dried mushrooms
4 oz./125 g. ham	4 oz. ham
2 pints/1 litre chicken stock	5 cups chicken stock
4 oz./125 g. chicken	4 oz. chicken
2 spring onions	2 scallions
1 teaspoon salt	1 teaspoon salt
1 tablespoon Vesop	1 tablespoon Vesop
1 tablespoon sherry	1 tablespoon sherry
½ teaspoon monosodium glutamate	½ teaspoon monosodium glutamate
pinch of pepper	pinch of pepper

METHOD

Cut the mushrooms into small pieces and soak in ½ pint
(¼ litre/1¼ cups) water for one hour. Bring the stock to
the boil.

Shred the ham and add to the stock. Simmer for 10
minutes. Add the mushrooms and their liquid. Slice the
chicken thinly, slice spring onions (scallions); add to the
stock. Simmer for 10 minutes.

Add the remaining ingredients, stir well and serve.

Ingredients for a mixed vegetable soup

RAINDROP SOUP

IMPERIAL/METRIC	AMERICAN
6 water chestnuts	*6 water chestnuts*
2 spring onions	*2 scallions*
1 tablespoon sherry	*1 tablespoon sherry*
salt and pepper	*salt and pepper*
1½ pints/¾ litre chicken stock	*3¾ cups chicken stock*
6 oz./180 g. diced cooked chicken	*1½ cups diced cooked chicken*

METHOD

Slice the water chestnuts and slice the spring onions (scallions) finely. Put these in a saucepan with the chicken stock and the chicken. Bring to the boil and simmer, covered, for 15 minutes.

Add the sherry and season to taste.

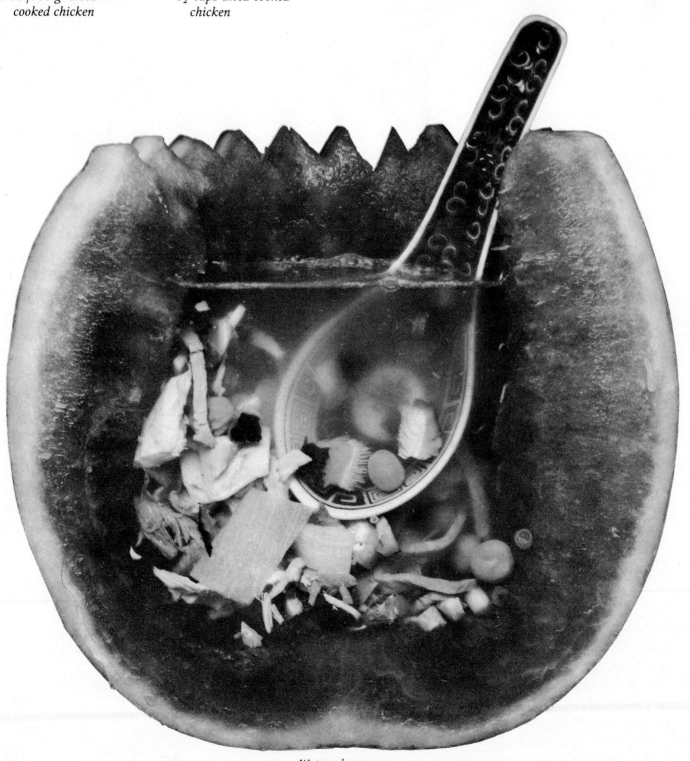

Watermelon soup

WATERMELON SOUP

IMPERIAL/METRIC	AMERICAN	METHOD
1 oz./30 g. dried mushrooms	1 oz. dried mushrooms	Cut the mushrooms into small pieces and soak in boiling water for 1 hour. Cut the bamboo shoots into thin slices; shred or mince (grind) the ham.
4 oz./125 g. bamboo shoots	4 oz. bamboo shoots	
4 oz./125 g. green peas	4 oz. green peas	Bring the stock to the boil. Mince (grind) the chicken and pork, add to the stock and simmer for 10 minutes. Add drained mushrooms, bamboo shoots and ham, mix well and add the monosodium glutamate and peas.
4 oz./125 g. lean ham	4 oz. lean ham	
1 pint/½ litre chicken stock	2½ cups chicken stock	
6 oz./180 g. chicken	6 oz. chicken	Cut the top from the melon and scoop out the seeds and some of the pulp. Pour the soup into the melon and replace the top. Stand the melon in a basin and steam for about 1½ hours or until the melon is cooked.
6 oz./180 g. pork	6 oz. pork	
½ teaspoon monosodium glutamate	½ teaspoon monosodium glutamate	The correct way to serve this soup is to place the melon on the table and scoop out soup and flesh, cutting the peel down as the level of soup is lowered.
4 lb./2 kg. watermelon	4 lb. watermelon	

CRAB AND VINEGAR SOUP

IMPERIAL/METRIC	AMERICAN	METHOD
1 large cooked crab	1 large cooked crab	Remove all the meat from the crab, discarding the sac and 'dead men's fingers'; chop the claw meat. Fry the meat in a little oil with the salt and ginger; slice the tomatoes, add to the crab and fry gently for 5 minutes. Add the chicken stock and simmer for 15 minutes.
1 teaspoon salt	1 teaspoon salt	
1 teaspoon chopped fresh ginger	1 teaspoon chopped fresh ginger	
2 tomatoes	2 tomatoes	
2 pints/1 litre chicken stock	5 cups chicken stock	
2 eggs	2 eggs	Beat the eggs and add to the soup in a thin stream, so that they form ribbons. Add the remaining ingredients, stir well and serve.
2 tablespoons sherry	2 tablespoons sherry	
2 tablespoons vinegar	2 tablespoons vinegar	
1 teaspoon salt	1 teaspoon salt	
2 tablespoons Vesop	2 tablespoons Vesop	
½ teaspoon monosodium glutamate	½ teaspoon monosodium glutamate	

SOUR SOUP

IMPERIAL/METRIC	AMERICAN	METHOD
2 pints/1 litre chicken stock	5 cups chicken stock	Bring the stock gently to the boil. Mix the soy sauce, cornflour (cornstarch), vinegar, salt, monosodium glutamate and pepper to a smooth paste. Add to the soup, stirring all the time until slightly thickened. Simmer for 5 minutes.
2 tablespoons soy sauce	2 tablespoons soy sauce	
2 tablespoons cornflour	2 tablespoons cornstarch	
3 tablespoons vinegar	¼ cup vinegar	
1 teaspoon salt	1 teaspoon salt	Beat the eggs until smooth and pour in a thin stream into the soup, so that they form ribbons. Add chopped meat or vegetables, if using.
½ teaspoon monosodium glutamate	½ teaspoon monosodium glutamate	
pinch of pepper	pinch of pepper	
3 eggs	3 eggs	
6 oz./180 g. chopped, cooked meat or vegetables, optional	6 oz. chopped, cooked meat or vegetables, optional	

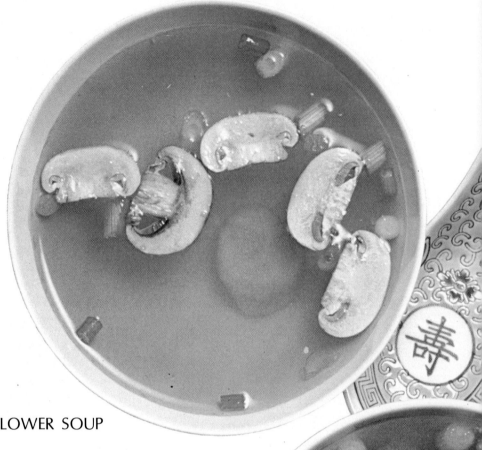

PRAWN (SHRIMP) AND EGG FLOWER SOUP

IMPERIAL/METRIC	AMERICAN
2 spring onions	2 scallions
$1\frac{1}{2}$ pints/$\frac{3}{4}$ litre chicken stock	$3\frac{3}{4}$ cups chicken stock
$\frac{1}{2}$ tablespoon dry sherry	$\frac{1}{2}$ tablespoon dry sherry
pinch of monosodium glutamate	pinch of monosodium glutamate
pinch of sugar	pinch of sugar
1 teaspoon soy sauce	1 teaspoon soy sauce
6 oz./180 g. peeled prawns	6 oz. peeled shrimp
1 egg, well beaten	1 egg, well beaten
salt	salt

METHOD

Chop the spring onions (scallions) finely and put them in a large saucepan with the stock. Bring to the boil and simmer, covered, for 10 minutes.

Add the sherry, monosodium glutamate, sugar, soy sauce and prawns (shrimp). Reheat gently until the prawns (shrimp) are heated through.

Pour in the egg and stir until it separates into shreds. Add salt to taste.

NOTE: King prawns should be deveined and halved.

BEEF AND VEGETABLE SOUP

IMPERIAL/METRIC
4 oz./125 g. topside of
  beef
1 tomato
2 spring onions
6 water chestnuts
4 oz./125 g. bamboo
  shoots
4 dried mushrooms
1½ pints/¾ litre beef stock
pinch of monosodium
  glutamate
salt and pepper

AMERICAN
4 oz. round of beef
1 tomato
2 scallions
6 water chestnuts
4 oz. bamboo shoots
4 dried mushrooms
3¾ cups beef stock
pinch of monosodium
  glutamate
salt and pepper

Mushroom soup (page 92);
Prawn (shrimp) and egg flower soup;
Beef and vegetable soup

METHOD
Cut the beef into thin strips across the grain of the meat.
Skin the tomato and slice into four. Slice the spring
onions (scallions), water chestnuts and bamboo shoots
into thin strips. Soak the mushrooms in warm water for
20 minutes, rinse, squeeze dry and cut into thin strips,
discarding the stalks.

Put the stock in a large saucepan and bring to the boil.
Add the beef and simmer for 4–5 minutes. Add the
vegetables and cook for 2 minutes. Add the monosodium
glutamate and season to taste.

MUSHROOM SOUP

IMPERIAL/METRIC	AMERICAN	METHOD
2 spring onions	2 scallions	Slice, thinly, the spring onions (scallions) and button mushrooms. Put the stock in a saucepan with the ginger and spring onions (scallions). Bring to the boil and simmer, covered, for 20 minutes.
4 oz./125 g. button mushrooms	4 oz. button mushrooms	
1½ pints/¾ litre chicken stock	3¾ cups chicken stock	Add the mushrooms and simmer for a further 10 minutes. Remove the ginger. Add the sherry and season to taste.
½ inch slice fresh ginger	½ inch slice fresh ginger	
1 tablespoon sherry	1 tablespoon sherry	

TOMATO SOUP WITH EGG FLOWER

IMPERIAL/METRIC	AMERICAN	METHOD
4 tomatoes	4 tomatoes	Skin and cut the tomatoes and cut the onion into eighths. Heat the oil in a large saucepan. Add the tomatoes and onion and fry for 5 minutes or until softened but not browned. Pour off excess oil and add the stock, salt and pepper and monosodium glutamate. Bring to the boil and simmer for 30 minutes.
1 onion	1 onion	
1 tablespoon oil	1 tablespoon oil	
1½ pints/¾ litre chicken stock	3¾ cups chicken stock	
pinch of monosodium glutamate	pinch of monosodium glutamate	Add the egg slowly, stirring constantly, until it separates into shreds.
salt and pepper	salt and pepper	
1 egg, beaten	1 egg, beaten	

CHINESE RAVIOLI SOUP

IMPERIAL/METRIC	AMERICAN	METHOD
2 pints/1 litre chicken stock	5 cups chicken stock	Bring the stock to the boil. Wash and chop the spring onions (scallions), add to the stock and simmer for 5 minutes. Add the salt, soy sauce and monosodium glutamate to the stock.
2 spring onions	2 scallions	
1 teaspoon salt	1 teaspoon salt	
1 tablespoon soy sauce	1 tablespoon soy sauce	Fry the ravioli in deep fat for 1–2 minutes or until crisp on the outside. Drain on kitchen paper. Put the ravioli in a large soup tureen and pour the stock over. The ravioli will rise to the top of the soup which must be served immediately in order for the crispness to be felt in contrast to the hot liquid.
½ teaspoon monosodium glutamate	½ teaspoon monosodium glutamate	
6 oz./180 g. Chinese ravioli	6 oz. Chinese ravioli	
deep fat for frying	deep fat for frying	

PORK AND WATERCRESS SOUP

IMPERIAL/METRIC	AMERICAN	METHOD
2 pints/1 litre bone stock	5 cups bone stock	Bring the stock to the boil and add the salt. Mix the cornflour (cornstarch) and water to a smooth paste, add the pork and mix well. Separate and add to the soup; simmer for 5 minutes.
1 teaspoon salt	1 teaspoon salt	
2 teaspoons cornflour	2 teaspoons cornstarch	
1 tablespoon water	1 tablespoon water	
4 oz./125 g. chopped pork	4 oz. chopped pork	Wash the watercress; wash and chop the spring onions (scallions); add to the stock with the remaining ingredients. Simmer for another 5 minutes.
1 bunch watercress	1 bunch watercress	
2 spring onions	2 scallions	
2 tablespoons soy sauce	2 tablespoons soy sauce	
½ teaspoon monosodium glutamate	½ teaspoon monosodium glutamate	
pinch of black pepper	pinch of black pepper	

Abalone and green pea soup

ABALONE AND GREEN PEA SOUP

IMPERIAL/METRIC
4 dried mushrooms
2 pints/1 litre pork stock
4 oz./125 g. lean pork
½ lb./250 g. fresh
    green peas or 4 oz./125 g.
    frozen peas, defrosted
1 small can abalone
1 tablespoon soy sauce

AMERICAN
4 dried mushrooms
5 cups pork stock
4 oz. lean pork
½ lb. fresh green peas
    or 4 oz. frozen peas,
    defrosted
1 small can abalone
1 tablespoon soy sauce

METHOD
Slice the mushrooms and soak in boiling water for 30 minutes.

Bring the stock to the boil. Shred the pork and add to the stock, simmering for 5 minutes. Add the peas and mushrooms and simmer for 5 minutes.

Drain the abalone, keeping the juice, and cut into small pieces; add to the stock with the juice and soy sauce. Stir and serve.

93

VEGETABLES

Many meat and fish dishes include vegetables in their ingredients and, conversely, many vegetable dishes have a small quantity of meat or seafood to give added flavour. Vegetables are an important part of a Chinese meal and one vegetable dish is usually served to every three meat, poultry and fish dishes.

The main characteristic of Chinese cooked vegetables is their crispness. Vegetables are usually shredded or cut into small pieces and cooked very quickly, with little or no liquid. Cooked in this way, each vegetable retains its own distinct flavour and texture.

Sometimes two cooking methods are employed, as in the case of hard vegetables, which are first fried for a couple of minutes and then have a little stock or water added to produce a combination of frying and braising; for quick frying over fierce heat the order can be reversed.

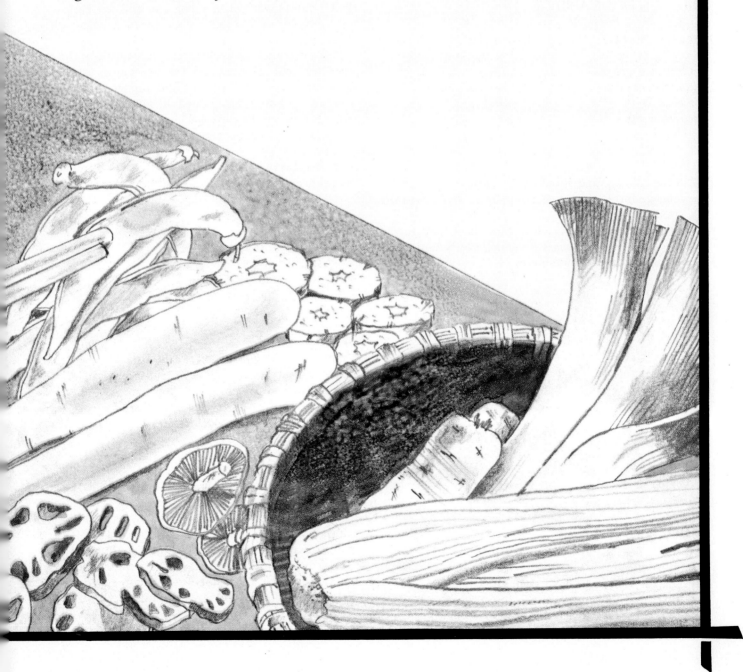

FRIED SPINACH

IMPERIAL/METRIC
2 lb./1 kg. fresh spinach,
  or ¾ lb./375 g. frozen
  leaf spinach
1 tablespoon oil
1 teaspoon salt
1 tablespoon soy sauce

AMERICAN
2 lb. fresh spinach, or
  ¾ lb. frozen leaf
  spinach
1 tablespoon oil
1 teaspoon salt
1 tablespoon soy sauce

METHOD
Wash the spinach thoroughly and drain off excess water, or defrost the frozen spinach. Heat the oil in a large saucepan, add the leaf spinach and fry over fierce heat for 1 minute, stirring all the time, until the spinach softens. Add the salt and soy sauce, mix well and cook gently for another minute.

FRIED CELERY CABBAGE

IMPERIAL/METRIC
1 lb./½ kg. white, or
  Chinese, cabbage
2 tablespoons oil or
  melted lard
1 teaspoon salt
2 sticks celery

AMERICAN
1 lb. white, or Chinese,
  cabbage
2 tablespoons oil or
  melted lard
1 teaspoon salt
2 sticks celery

METHOD
Wash the cabbage and shred finely. Heat the oil and fry the cabbage for 3 minutes, stirring all the time. Add the salt, mixing well.

Wash the celery and cut into thin slices, add to the cabbage with 2 tablespoons water; cook over a fierce heat, stirring all the time, for 2 minutes.

CELERY AND MUSHROOMS

IMPERIAL/METRIC
1 small head celery
½ lb./250 g. fresh
  mushrooms
2 tablespoons oil or
  melted lard
1 teaspoon salt
1 teaspoon brown sugar
2 tablespoons soy sauce
1 teaspoon Vesop

AMERICAN
1 small head celery
½ lb. fresh mushrooms
2 tablespoons oil or
  melted lard
1 teaspoon salt
1 teaspoon brown sugar
2 tablespoons soy sauce
1 teaspoon Vesop

METHOD
Wash the celery and cut into 1 inch lengths. Wash the mushrooms and cut into thick slices. Heat the oil and fry the mushrooms for 1 minute, add the celery, salt, sugar, soy sauce and Vesop, mix well and cook for 5 minutes.

SWEET AND SOUR CABBAGE

IMPERIAL/METRIC
1 large carrot
3 tomatoes
3 tablespoons oil or
  melted lard
1 tablespoon cornflour
¼ pint/1 dcl. stock or
  water
2 tablespoons soy sauce
1 teaspoon salt
1 tablespoon brown sugar
2 tablespoons wine vinegar
1 white, or Chinese,
  cabbage
2 tablespoons sherry

AMERICAN
1 large carrot
3 tomatoes
¼ cup oil or melted lard
1 tablespoon cornstarch
¾ cup stock or water
2 tablespoons soy sauce
1 teaspoon salt
1 tablespoon brown sugar
2 tablespoons wine vinegar
1 white, or Chinese,
  cabbage
2 tablespoons sherry

METHOD
Peel and shred or grate the carrot; chop the tomatoes. Heat 1 tablespoon oil in a pan and add the carrots and tomatoes; fry for 2–3 minutes over medium heat, stirring constantly.

Mix the cornflour (cornstarch) with a little of the stock or water, add the rest and the soy sauce, salt, brown sugar and vinegar. Add to the tomato mixture and bring to the boil, stirring until thickened. Simmer gently while preparing the cabbage.

Shred the cabbage and fry in the remaining oil in another large pan, for 3–4 minutes, stirring constantly. Add the sherry, mix well and cook for 2 minutes. Pile the cabbage on to a dish and pour the sauce over.

CABBAGE WITH CRAB SAUCE

IMPERIAL/METRIC
1 lb./½ kg. white
  cabbage
1 tablespoon oil
1 clove garlic
1 tablespoon soy sauce
1 tablespoon sherry
1 teaspoon cornflour
2 tablespoons stock or
  cabbage water
4 oz./125 g. canned crab meat

AMERICAN
1 lb. white cabbage
1 tablespoon oil
1 clove garlic
1 tablespoon soy sauce
1 tablespoon sherry
1 teaspoon cornstarch
2 tablespoons stock or
  cabbage water
4 oz. canned crab meat

METHOD
Wash and shred the cabbage. Cook in salted, boiling water for 2 minutes. Drain, reserving 2 tablespoons water if no stock is available. Heat the oil and fry the cabbage and crushed garlic for 2 minutes. Add the soy sauce and sherry, mix well and cook for 1 minute.

Mix the cornflour (cornstarch) to a smooth paste with the stock or cabbage water, stir into the pan with the crab. Mix well and cook for 1 minute.

Sweet and sour cabbage

CHINESE PICKLED CUCUMBER

IMPERIAL/METRIC	AMERICAN
1 cucumber	*1 cucumber*
2 tablespoons vinegar	*2 tablespoons vinegar*
1 tablespoon brown sugar	*1 tablespoon brown sugar*
1 teaspoon ground ginger	*1 teaspoon ground ginger*
1 teaspoon sesame oil,	*1 teaspoon sesame oil,*
optional	*optional*

METHOD

Peel the cucumber and cut into thin slices. Put the vinegar, sugar and ginger in a small pan, bring to the boil, pour over the cucumber and leave until cold.

Stir in sesame oil, if using, at the last minute.

BRAISED BEAN SPROUTS

IMPERIAL/METRIC	AMERICAN
1 lb./½ kg. bean sprouts	*1 lb. bean sprouts*
1 tablespoon oil	*1 tablespoon oil*
1 teaspoon vinegar	*1 teaspoon vinegar*
pinch of salt	*pinch of salt*
1 tablespoon soy sauce,	*1 tablespoon soy sauce,*
optional	*optional*

METHOD

Wash the bean sprouts and dry well. Heat the oil and fry the sprouts over a fierce heat for 3 minutes, stirring all the time. Add the remaining ingredients; mix well.

FRIED LETTUCE

IMPERIAL/METRIC	AMERICAN
1 large lettuce	*1 large lettuce*
1 tablespoon oil	*1 tablespoon oil*
2 cloves garlic	*2 cloves garlic*
pinch of salt	*pinch of salt*
1 teaspoon Vesop	*1 teaspoon Vesop*

METHOD

Wash and trim the lettuce and shake off excess moisture. Cut into four. Heat the oil and fry the lettuce for 1 minute. Add the crushed garlic, salt and Vesop; mix well and cook for another minute.

VEGETABLES WITH SWEET AND SOUR SAUCE

IMPERIAL/METRIC	AMERICAN
1 small red pepper	*1 small red pepper*
1 small green pepper	*1 small green pepper*
1 onion	*1 onion*
1 carrot	*1 carrot*
2 sticks celery	*2 sticks celery*
1 tablespoon cornflour	*1 tablespoon cornstarch*
1 tablespoon soy sauce	*1 tablespoon soy sauce*
4 tablespoons brown sugar	*⅓ cup brown sugar*
¼ pint/1 dcl. chicken stock	*¾ cup chicken stock*
4 tablespoons vinegar	*⅓ cup vinegar*
salt	*salt*

METHOD

Cut the peppers into wedges, the onion into eighths and the carrot into wedges. Slice the celery diagonally. Drop the vegetables into boiling water and simmer for 5 minutes. Mix the cornflour (cornstarch) with the soy sauce. Put the sugar, stock and vinegar in a saucepan, bring to the boil and add cornflour (cornstarch) and soy sauce. Simmer, stirring, for 2–3 minutes. Add the vegetables and salt to taste and reheat. Serve in a heated bowl.

BRAISED TURNIPS

IMPERIAL/METRIC	AMERICAN
1 lb./½ kg. young turnips	*1 lb. young turnips*
2 tablespoons oil or	*2 tablespoons oil or*
melted lard	*melted lard*
2 spring onions	*2 scallions*
¼ pint/1 dcl. stock	*¾ cup stock*
1 teaspoon meat extract	*1 teaspoon meat extract*
2 tablespoons soy sauce	*2 tablespoons soy sauce*
1 teaspoon brown sugar	*1 teaspoon brown sugar*
pinch of black pepper	*pinch of black pepper*

METHOD

Thickly peel the turnips and cut them into small dice. Heat the oil or lard and fry the turnips for 3 minutes. Chop the spring onions (scallions) and add to the pan, mix well. Add the stock, meat extract, soy sauce and sugar; mix well. Cover the pan and simmer for 5 minutes. Sprinkle with black pepper.

FRIED MUSHROOMS AND BAMBOO SHOOTS

IMPERIAL/METRIC	AMERICAN
12 dried mushrooms	12 dried mushrooms
2 tablespoons oil	2 tablespoons oil
½ lb./250 g. bamboo shoots	½ lb. bamboo shoots
pinch of salt	pinch of salt
2 tablespoons sherry	2 tablespoons sherry
1 teaspoon Vesop	1 teaspoon Vesop
1 tablespoon cornflour	1 tablespoon cornstarch
4 oz./125 g. minced ham	4 oz. ground ham

METHOD
Soak the mushrooms in boiling water for 30 minutes. Drain and slice. Heat the oil and fry the mushrooms for 3 minutes. Remove from the pan.

Drain the bamboo shoots and cut into slices, add to the remaining oil with the salt, sherry and Vesop. Bring gently to the boil and simmer for 3 minutes.

Mix the cornflour (cornstarch) to a smooth paste with a little of the mushroom water, make up to ¼ pint (1 dcl./ ¾ cup) and add to the pan with the mushrooms; cover and simmer for 10 minutes. Arrange on a large dish and sprinkle with ham.

BRAISED CABBAGE WITH MUSHROOMS

IMPERIAL/METRIC	AMERICAN
1 lb./½ kg. white, or Chinese, cabbage	1 lb. white, or Chinese, cabbage
2 tablespoons peanut oil	2 tablespoons peanut oil
1 green pepper	1 green pepper
1 tablespoon soy sauce	1 tablespoon soy sauce
1 teaspoon sugar	1 teaspoon sugar
pinch of monosodium glutamate	pinch of monosodium glutamate
4 oz./125 g. button mushrooms	4 oz. button mushrooms
salt and pepper	salt and pepper

METHOD
Clean the cabbage and chop it roughly. Heat the oil in a saucepan, add the cabbage and fry it for 2–3 minutes, stirring constantly. Cut the pepper into strips and add to the pan with the soy sauce, sugar, monosodium glutamate and mushrooms. Season. Add 4 tablespoons (⅓ cup) water, cover the pan and cook for 5–7 minutes, shaking the pan occasionally.

Braised cabbage with mushrooms

STUFFED PEPPERS

IMPERIAL/METRIC	AMERICAN
4 green peppers	4 green peppers
1 lb./½ kg. lean pork, cooked and minced	1 lb. lean pork, cooked and ground
1 clove garlic	1 clove garlic
1 tablespoon soy sauce	1 tablespoon soy sauce
1 tablespoon cornflour	1 tablespoon cornstarch
1 tablespoon sherry	1 tablespoon sherry

METHOD
Wash and core the peppers; keeping them whole; remove the seeds. Put peppers in a large pan, cover with cold water, bring to the boil and drain.

Mix the pork, crushed garlic, soy sauce, cornflour (cornstarch) and sherry together, until blended. Fill the peppers with the pork mixture; place in a greased dish, cover and steam for 30 minutes.

BROCCOLI WITH PORK

IMPERIAL/METRIC	AMERICAN
¾ lb./375 g. cooked or frozen broccoli	¾ lb. cooked or frozen broccoli
2 tablespoons peanut oil	2 tablespoons peanut oil
1 teaspoon sugar	1 teaspoon sugar
pinch of salt	pinch of salt
½ teaspoon very finely chopped fresh ginger	½ teaspoon very finely chopped fresh ginger
1 clove garlic, crushed	1 clove garlic, crushed
2 tablespoons soy sauce	2 tablespoons soy sauce
1 tablespoon sherry	1 tablespoon sherry
1 teaspoon cornflour	1 teaspoon cornstarch
4 oz./125 g. thinly sliced cooked pork	1 cup thinly sliced cooked pork

METHOD

Cut the broccoli into 1½ inch lengths. Heat the oil in a saucepan, add the broccoli and fry for 2–3 minutes. Add the sugar, salt, ginger and garlic, cover the pan and cook slowly for 4–5 minutes.

Mix the soy sauce, sherry and cornflour (cornstarch) with 3 tablespoons (¼ cup) water. Stir this in to the saucepan, cover again and cook for a further 3–4 minutes. Add the pork and reheat.

CAULIFLOWER, WATER CHESTNUTS AND MUSHROOMS

IMPERIAL/METRIC	AMERICAN
1 small cauliflower	1 small cauliflower
8 water chestnuts	8 water chestnuts
6 dried mushrooms	6 dried mushrooms
2 tablespoons oil	2 tablespoons oil
2 tablespoons cornflour	2 tablespoons cornstarch
2 tablespoons soy sauce	2 tablespoons soy sauce
2 tablespoons sherry	2 tablespoons sherry
2 tablespoons stock	2 tablespoons stock

METHOD

Wash the cauliflower and break into florets, cover with boiling water and leave for 5 minutes. Drain. Cut the chestnuts into large pieces.

Cover the mushrooms with ½ pint (¼ litre/1¼ cups) boiling water, cover and leave for 30 minutes. Drain, reserve the water; cut the mushrooms into thin slices. Heat the oil and fry the mushrooms for 2–3 minutes over fierce heat, stirring constantly. Add the chestnuts and cauliflower, mix well and cook for 2 minutes.

Mix the cornflour (cornstarch) to a smooth paste with the remaining ingredients, add the mushroom water. Add to the pan and bring to the boil, stirring, until thickened. Cook for 2–3 minutes.

BEAN CURD WITH OYSTER SAUCE

IMPERIAL/METRIC	AMERICAN
4 oz./125 g. fresh mushrooms	4 oz. fresh mushrooms
2 tablespoons oil	2 tablespoons oil
1 lb./½ kg. bean curd	1 lb. bean curd
3 tablespoons oyster sauce	¼ cup oyster sauce
pinch of black pepper	pinch of black pepper

METHOD

Wash and slice the mushrooms. Heat the oil and fry the mushrooms over fierce heat for 2 minutes, stirring constantly. Remove them from the pan.

Break the bean curd into small pieces and add to the remaining oil, cook gently for 2–3 minutes until browned on the outside. Add the oyster sauce and pepper, mix well and leave for 2 minutes. Add the mushrooms, mix well and gently heat through.

COLD SWEET AND SOUR RADISHES

IMPERIAL/METRIC	AMERICAN
2 bunches small radishes	2 bunches small radishes
1 teaspoon salt	1 teaspoon salt
2 tablespoons soy sauce	2 tablespoons soy sauce
1 tablespoon wine vinegar	1 tablespoon wine vinegar
1 tablespoon brown sugar	1 tablespoon brown sugar
2 teaspoons sesame oil	2 teaspoons sesame oil

METHOD

Wash, top and tail the radishes; drain. Using the handle of a heavy kitchen knife, smash each radish, but do not break them completely – they must remain almost whole. Sprinkle with salt and leave for 5 minutes. Add the remaining ingredients, mix well and, when the sugar has dissolved, mix again.

COLD ASPARAGUS

IMPERIAL/METRIC	AMERICAN
1 lb./½ kg. asparagus	1 lb. asparagus
2 tablespoons soy sauce	2 tablespoons soy sauce
1 teaspoon brown sugar	1 teaspoon brown sugar
1 tablespoon olive oil	1 tablespoon olive oil
pinch of salt	pinch of salt

METHOD

Wash the asparagus and cut off the tough part of the stems. Put into a large pan, cover with boiling water and bring back to the boil. Simmer for 5 minutes. Drain. Rinse immediately under cold running water until completely cold. Drain well.

Put asparagus in a serving dish, add the soy sauce, sugar, oil and salt, mix well and serve as a salad.

COLD CUCUMBER

IMPERIAL/METRIC	AMERICAN
1 cucumber	1 cucumber
½ teaspoon salt	½ teaspoon salt
1 tablespoon soy sauce	1 tablespoon soy sauce
1 tablespoon wine vinegar	1 tablespoon wine vinegar
1 tablespoon caster sugar	1 tablespoon powdered sugar
2 teaspoons sesame oil	2 teaspoons sesame oil

METHOD
Peel the cucumber and cut into small dice. Sprinkle with the remaining ingredients and leave for 5 minutes before serving. Make sure the sugar has dissolved before serving.

COLD CELERY

IMPERIAL/METRIC	AMERICAN
1 head celery	1 head celery
pinch of salt	pinch of salt
1 tablespoon soy sauce	1 tablespoon soy sauce
1 teaspoon brown sugar	1 teaspoon brown sugar
1 teaspoon sesame oil	1 teaspoon sesame oil

METHOD
Scrub the celery and cut into 1 inch lengths. Put into a large pan, cover with cold water, bring to the boil, drain and immediately cover with cold water. Chill completely under cold running water. Drain. Add the salt, soy sauce, sugar and sesame oil.

Mix well and serve very cold.

Cold asparagus, sweet and sour radishes, cucumber and celery

RICE

Although rice is a staple food of China, it is not eaten with every dish as is commonly believed in the West. A meal of about eight dishes will usually include one rice dish. It is usually steamed or boiled and has a dry, fluffy consistency. Fried rice, popular in the West, originated as a way of using up leftover rice and it has since become a dish in itself, with a variety of ingredients added.

& NOODLES

Another staple food of the Chinese, after rice and dumplings, is noodles. Most Chinese noodles are made from wheat flour, but there are also rice flour and pea starch noodles, the latter being used mainly in soups. They vary in thickness from that of macaroni to the finest vermicelli. Crispy noodles are obtained by frying; soft noodles are boiled and usually prepared with a sauce or gravy.

If possible, make your own noodles from the recipe in this chapter or buy fresh noodles from a Chinese store. Otherwise, Italian noodles will serve equally well for most recipes, but follow the instructions on the packet as they may take a little longer to cook than Chinese noodles.

STEAMED RICE

IMPERIAL/METRIC	AMERICAN
4 oz./125 g. long grain rice	$\frac{2}{3}$ cup long grain rice
$1\frac{1}{2}$–2 pints/$\frac{3}{4}$–1 litre water	$3\frac{3}{4}$–5 cups water

METHOD

Wash and drain the rice. Cook in boiling water for 3 minutes. Drain. Put the rice in a steaming tier and cook for 30 minutes. (If no steaming tier is available, use a nylon or hair sieve in a wooden band.)

BOILED RICE

IMPERIAL/METRIC	AMERICAN
$\frac{1}{2}$ lb./250 g. long grain rice	$1\frac{1}{3}$ cups long grain rice
$\frac{3}{4}$ pint/$3\frac{1}{2}$ dcl. water	2 cups water

METHOD

Wash and drain the rice. Cook in boiling water for 5 minutes, stirring occasionally to prevent sticking.

Reduce the heat to simmering, cover the pan and cook for 20 minutes or until all the water has been absorbed and the grains are quite separate.

FRIED RICE

IMPERIAL/METRIC	AMERICAN
$\frac{3}{4}$ lb./375 g. cooked, cold rice	$\frac{3}{4}$ lb. cooked, cold rice
2 tablespoons oil	2 tablespoons oil
2 eggs	2 eggs

METHOD

Season the rice well with salt and black pepper. Heat the oil and fry the rice gently over medium heat for about 10 minutes, or until all fat has been absorbed.

Beat the eggs until smooth and pour on to the rice in a thin stream, stirring all the time. Heat gently, stirring, until the egg is evenly distributed and set.

NOTE: This is the simplest form of fried rice, which, although very popular in the West, is not served in restaurants in China, and rarely in the home.

FRIED RICE WITH CHICKEN

IMPERIAL/METRIC	AMERICAN
2 tablespoons oil	2 tablespoons oil
2 spring onions	2 scallions
1 clove garlic, crushed	1 clove garlic, crushed
$\frac{3}{4}$ lb./375 g. cooked rice	$\frac{3}{4}$ lb. cooked rice
$\frac{1}{2}$ lb./250 g. cooked chicken	$\frac{1}{2}$ lb. cooked chicken
2 tablespoons soy sauce	2 tablespoons soy sauce
2 eggs	2 eggs
salt and pepper	salt and pepper

METHOD

Heat the oil; peel and finely chop the onions; fry the spring onions (scallions) and garlic in the oil for 2 minutes over a medium heat. Add the rice, mix well and heat through.

Chop the chicken and mix with the soy sauce, add to the rice mixture and mix well. Beat the eggs until smooth, season with salt and pepper. Pour into the rice mixture in a thin steam, stirring all the time, until the eggs are cooked.

Fried rice with pork and shrimps

FRIED RICE WITH PORK AND SHRIMPS

Follow the recipe for fried rice with chicken, substituting 6 oz./180 g. chopped, cooked pork and 4 oz./125 g. cooked shrimps for the chicken.

FRIED RICE WITH HAM AND BEAN SPROUTS

Follow the recipe for fried rice with chicken, substituting 6 oz./180 g. chopped ham for the chicken and stirring in $\frac{1}{2}$ lb./250 g. drained bean sprouts.

FRIED RICE WITH CRAB AND BAMBOO SHOOTS

Follow the recipe for fried rice with chicken, substituting 7 oz./200 g. crab meat and 4 oz./125 g. bamboo shoots, finely sliced, for the chicken.

FRIED RICE WITH PRAWNS (SHRIMP) AND WATER CHESTNUTS

Follow the recipe for fried rice with chicken, substituting for the chicken 4 oz./125 g. chopped prawns (shrimp) and 4 chopped water chestnuts.

NOODLE PASTE

IMPERIAL/METRIC	AMERICAN
1 egg	1 egg
$\frac{1}{2}$ lb./250 g. plain flour	2 cups all-purpose flour
pinch of salt	pinch of salt

METHOD

Sift the flour and salt into a mixing bowl. Make a well in the centre and add the egg. Using a round-bladed knife, mix the flour into the egg and add enough water to make a stiff dough. Knead with the hand, very thoroughly. Roll out dough as thinly as possible on a lightly floured board.

Hun t'un: Cut into 2–3 inch squares.
Dumplings: Cut into 4 inch diameter rounds.
Noodles: Lightly flour the dough, roll up like a Swiss roll and slice into $\frac{1}{16}-\frac{1}{8}$ inch slices. Unroll and hang over the back of a chair (on a clean tea towel) for about 20 minutes, to dry out.

For soft noodles, boil for 5–7 minutes in a large saucepan of salted boiling water.

For crisp noodles, fry in deep, hot oil until golden and drain well. There is no need to boil the noodles before frying, as with bought noodles.

SZECHUAN NOODLES

IMPERIAL/METRIC	AMERICAN
4 oz./125 g. peeled prawns, chopped	1 cup peeled shrimp, chopped
1 oz. ham, shredded	1 oz. ham, shredded
1 stick celery, chopped	1 stick celery, chopped
1 teaspoon fresh ginger	1 teaspoon fresh ginger
2 oz./60 g. minced cooked pork	$\frac{1}{4}$ cup ground cooked pork
2 tablespoons peanut oil	2 tablespoons peanut oil
2 tablespoons brandy	2 tablespoons brandy
$\frac{1}{2}$ teaspoon chilli sauce	$\frac{1}{2}$ teaspoon chili sauce
1 tablespoon tomato sauce	1 tablespoon tomato sauce
1 tablespoon soy sauce	1 tablespoon soy sauce
1 tablespoon cornflour	1 tablespoon cornstarch
3 tablespoons chicken stock	$\frac{1}{4}$ cup chicken stock
salt and pepper to taste	salt and pepper to taste
$\frac{1}{2}$ lb./250 g. dried egg, or home-made, noodles	$\frac{1}{2}$ lb. dried egg, or home-made, noodles

METHOD

Mix together the prawns (shrimp), ham, celery and pork. Heat the oil, add the pork mixture and fry, stirring, for 3–4 minutes. Add the ginger, finely chopped, the brandy, sauces, cornflour (cornstarch), stock and seasoning. Cook for 7–8 minutes, stirring constantly. Keep hot. Cook noodles in boiling salted water until tender. Drain and arrange on a serving plate; top with the sauce.

CRISPY NOODLES
WITH CHICKEN AND VEGETABLES

IMPERIAL/METRIC	AMERICAN
$\frac{1}{2}$ lb./250 g. dried egg, or home-made noodles	$\frac{1}{2}$ lb. dried egg, or home-made, noodles
3 tablespoons peanut oil	$\frac{1}{4}$ cup peanut oil
6 oz./180 g. cooked chicken	$1\frac{1}{2}$ cups cooked chicken
2 dried mushrooms	2 dried mushrooms
2 spring onions	2 scallions
1 tablespoon soy sauce	1 tablespoon soy sauce
pinch of monosodium glutamate	pinch of monosodium glutamate
pinch of sugar	pinch of sugar
$\frac{1}{2}$ teaspoon salt	$\frac{1}{2}$ teaspoon salt
$2\frac{1}{2}$ oz./75 g. bamboo shoots	$2\frac{1}{2}$ oz. bamboo shoots
2 sticks celery	2 sticks celery
1 carrot	1 carrot
2 tablespoons chicken stock	2 tablespoons chicken stock
$\frac{1}{4}$ inch slice fresh ginger	$\frac{1}{4}$ inch slice fresh ginger
1 teaspoon cornflour	1 teaspoon cornstarch
oil for deep frying	oil for deep frying

METHOD
If using bought noodles, loosen them, and cook in salted boiling water for 10 minutes, and drain well. Home-made noodles do not need boiling. Stir 1 tablespoon oil into the noodles. Cut the chicken into strips. Soak the mushrooms in warm water for 20 minutes, rinse, squeeze dry and slice thinly, discarding the stalks. Chop the spring onions (scallions) finely.

Mix the soy sauce, monosodium glutamate, sugar and salt in a bowl. Add the chicken and spring onions (scallions); stir and leave for 20 minutes.

Cut the bamboo shoots into thin strips, slice the celery diagonally and cut the carrot into wedges.

Heat the remaining oil in a frying pan (skillet) with the ginger. Remove the ginger, add the prepared vegetables and fry for 5 minutes, stirring constantly. Add the chicken and stock, mixed with cornflour (cornstarch). Bring to the boil, stirring constantly; simmer for 2–3 minutes. Keep hot.

Deep fry the noodles in hot oil until crisp and golden. Drain well on absorbent kitchen paper. Serve the noodles in a heated serving bowl, topped with the chicken and vegetable mixture.

HUN T'UN
WITH CHICKEN AND PRAWN FILLING

IMPERIAL/METRIC	AMERICAN
24 hun t'un skins or $\frac{1}{2}$ the recipe for noodle paste	24 hun t'un skins or $\frac{1}{2}$ the recipe for noodle paste
$\frac{1}{2}$ lb./250 g. cooked minced chicken	2 cups cooked ground chicken
$\frac{1}{2}$ lb./250 g. peeled prawns	2 cups peeled shrimp
2 spring onions	2 scallions
pinch of sugar	pinch of sugar
pinch of salt and pepper	pinch of salt and pepper
pinch of monosodium glutamate	pinch of monosodium glutamate
1 tablespoon soy sauce	1 tablespoon soy sauce
egg yolk	egg yolk
oil for deep frying	oil for deep frying

METHOD
Mince (grind) or chop finely the chicken, prawns (shrimp) and spring onions (scallions). Add the sugar, salt, pepper, monosodium glutamate and soy sauce and mix thoroughly.

Divide this filling evenly between the paste squares. Spread the filling over each square and roll it up like a Swiss roll, folding in the ends. Seal the edges with egg yolk. Deep fry in hot oil until golden. Drain well on absorbent kitchen paper and serve as soon as possible with pungent sauce.

Pungent sauce: Mix together 2 tablespoons sugar, 2 tablespoons vinegar, 1 teaspoon soy sauce, $\frac{1}{2}$ teaspoon very finely chopped fresh ginger, 1 teaspoon tomato paste, $\frac{1}{4}$ teaspoon salt, $\frac{1}{4}$ pint (1 dcl./$\frac{3}{4}$ cup) water and 1 tablespoon cornflour (cornstarch).

Bring to the boil, stirring constantly, and simmer for 2–3 minutes.

HUN T'UN
WITH PORK AND MUSHROOMS FILLING

Follow above recipe but use, instead of chicken and prawns (shrimp), 12 oz./375 g. minced (ground) cooked pork and 6 dried mushrooms. Soak the mushrooms in warm water for 20 minutes, rinse, squeeze dry, discarding stalks, and fry for 2–3 minutes in a little peanut oil before mincing.

HUN T'UN
WITH PORK AND VEGETABLES FILLING

Follow above recipe but use, instead of mushrooms, 4 oz./125 g. shredded spinach, 4 water chestnuts and 2 sticks celery.

Some of the ingredients which may be added to fried rice and hun t'un fillings

WOR MEIN

IMPERIAL/METRIC	AMERICAN
½ lb./250 g. dried egg, or home-made, noodles	½ lb. dried egg, or home-made, noodles
6 oz./180 g. pork	6 oz. pork
1 carrot	1 carrot
1 onion	1 onion
2 dried mushrooms	2 dried mushrooms
2 tablespoons peanut oil	2 tablespoons peanut oil
¼ pint/1 dcl. chicken stock	¾ cup chicken stock
1 tablespoon cornflour	1 tablespoon cornstarch
1 tablespoon soy sauce	1 tablespoon soy sauce
6 hard-boiled eggs	6 hard-cooked eggs
salt	salt

METHOD

Cook dried egg noodles (loosened) in salted boiling water for 15–20 minutes, until soft. Cook home-made noodles for 5–7 minutes. Drain and keep hot.

Cut the pork into thin strips, the carrot into wedges and the onion into eighths. Soak the mushrooms in warm water for 20 minutes, rinse, squeeze dry and slice; discard the stalks. Heat the oil in a saucepan; add the pork and fry until browned, stirring constantly. Add the vegetables, cover and cook gently for 10 minutes.

Mix together the stock, cornflour (cornstarch), soy sauce and salt to taste. Add to pan, bring to the boil, stirring, and simmer for 1–2 minutes.

Arrange noodles in 6 individual serving bowls. Place the pork mixture on top and serve, garnished with quarters of hard-boiled egg.

STEAMED DUMPLINGS

½ the recipe for noodle paste
one of the fillings for hun t'un

METHOD

Roll out the noodle dough and cut it into 4 inch diameter rounds. Using any of the fillings given for hun t'un, place mixture on the rounds and either fold over the dough to make a semi-circle (like a turnover) or gather up the edges into a small bunch on top. Seal the opening well with egg yolk.

Place each dumpling on a piece of greaseproof (waxed) paper and pack closely in one layer in a steamer or heatproof bowl. Place steamer over gently boiling water or the heatproof bowl in a pan of simmering water coming halfway up the sides. Cover closely and steam steadily for 25–30 minutes.

DIM SUM

While most of the recipes in this book fall into clearly defined categories, those in this chapter do not, so we have put them under the general heading of *dim sum*. The literal meaning of this phrase is 'dot the heart', but a rough translation could be 'fill a gap', for dim sum are snacks which can be eaten between meals. They may be served on their own at any time of the day or as an accompaniment to meals.

The recipes include steamed rolls, fried onion cakes and the famous spring rolls – so called because they are eaten in the spring, soon after the Chinese New Year, which generally falls in February.

STEAMED ROLLS

IMPERIAL/METRIC	AMERICAN
½ oz./15 g. fresh yeast	½ oz. fresh yeast
1 pint/6 dcl. warm water	2½ cups warm water
1½ lb./700 g. plain flour	1½ lb. all-purpose flour
salt	salt
oil	oil

METHOD

Cream the yeast and add to the water, knead into the flour until smooth and elastic; this takes about 5 minutes. Put into a clean bowl and leave, covered, in a warm place for about 1½ hours or until the dough has doubled its original size.

Turn on to a floured surface and knead lightly. Divide into two pieces and roll out each to an oblong about 15 inches long by 4 inches wide. Sprinkle with salt and oil. Roll each piece up from the long side to make two sausage shapes. Cut each into short lengths and leave in a warm place for about 10 minutes.

Steam the rolls in a steaming tier for 20 minutes.

NOTE: These rolls can successfully be stored in a cold place and reheated without loss of flavour or texture.

FRIED HUN T'UN

IMPERIAL/METRIC	AMERICAN
1 lb./½ kg. hun t'un paste	1 lb. hun t'un paste
1 lb./½ kg. streaky pork	1 lb. streaky pork
2 tablespoons soy sauce	2 tablespoons soy sauce
1 teaspoon brown sugar	1 teaspoon brown sugar
1 teaspoon salt	1 teaspoon salt
¾ lb./375 g. frozen leaf spinach	¾ lb. frozen leaf spinach
deep fat for frying	deep fat for frying

METHOD

Cut out 2 inch rounds from the paste. Mince (grind) the pork, add soy sauce, sugar and salt, mix well and leave for 10 minutes. Defrost the spinach and squeeze in a clean, dry cloth to get rid of excess moisture. Add the pork and mix well.

Place a little of the mixture in the centre of each round, dampen the edges and press together to seal. Drop the hun t'un into deep fat and fry for about 5 minutes, turning during cooking to brown evenly.

Drain and serve hot.

NOTE: Hun t'un paste, or skin as it is sometimes called, is usually available from most Chinese stores. The correct pronunciation is 'one ton'.

PASTIES

IMPERIAL/METRIC	AMERICAN
¾ lb./375 g. minced beef	¾ lb. ground beef
4 tablespoons oil	¼ cup oil
6 spring onions	6 scallions
4 oz./125 g. white cabbage heart	4 oz. white cabbage heart
1 tablespoon soy sauce	1 tablespoon soy sauce
1 teaspoon salt	1 teaspoon salt
¾ lb./340 g. plain flour	3 cups all-purpose flour
1 egg	1 egg
½ pint/3 dcl. water	1¼ cups water
¼ pint/1½ dcl. hot stock or water	¾ cup hot stock or water

METHOD

Fry the beef in the oil for 10 minutes. Chop the spring onions (scallions) and cabbage finely, add to the pan and cook for 2–3 minutes. Add the soy sauce and salt, mix well and leave until cold.

Mix the flour and egg together with enough water to make a soft dough. Turn on to a floured surface and knead lightly. Roll out very thinly and cut into 3 inch rounds. Place a little of the mixture in the centre of each round; dampen the edges with water and press together to seal.

Fry the pasties in the oil for 3 minutes, turning them once during cooking. Add the hot stock or water, cover the pan and simmer for 5 minutes.

From top: Steamed rolls; Fried hun t'un; Pasties; Boiled pastry balls

BOILED PASTRY BALLS

IMPERIAL/METRIC	AMERICAN
½ lb./250 g. lean pork	½ lb. lean pork
2 tablespoons soy sauce	2 tablespoons soy sauce
1 teaspoon sherry	1 teaspoon sherry
1 spring onion	1 scallion
few drops sesame oil	few drops sesame oil
1 tablespoon cornflour	1 tablespoon cornstarch
pinch of salt	pinch of salt
½ lb./225 g. rice flour	2 cups rice flour
about ¼ pint/1½ dcl. hot water	about ¾ cup hot water

METHOD

Mince (grind) the pork and mix in the soy sauce and sherry. Chop the spring onion (scallion) finely and add to the pork with the sesame oil, cornflour (cornstarch) and salt. Beat well until blended.

Mix the flour and hot water together to make a soft dough, adding more water if necessary. Divide the dough into 24 pieces and shape each into a ball. Make a hole in the centre of each ball and press some of the pork filling into the middle. Shape the dough around the filling and pinch the edges together. Drop the balls into a large pan of salted boiling water, allow to come back to the boil and boil for 5 minutes. Add ½ pint (¼ litre/1¼ cups) cold water to the pan, bring back to the boil and boil for another 3 minutes.

Drain the balls and serve four or more to each person with a little of the boiling water. Use a spoon to eat the balls, in order to catch the juices from the centre as the first bite is taken.

EGG ROLLS

IMPERIAL/METRIC	AMERICAN
6 eggs	6 eggs
3 oz./85 g. flour	¾ cup flour
½ pint/3 dcl. water	1¼ cups water
filling as for spring rolls	filling as for spring rolls
deep fat for frying	deep fat for frying

METHOD

Beat the eggs, flour and water together to make a smooth batter. Using a heavy-based 10 inch frying pan (skillet), make thin pancakes, cooking each on one side only.

Place a spoonful of filling in the centre and roll into parcels as for spring rolls. Deep fry the rolls for about 5 minutes, turning each during cooking to brown evenly.

Drain and cut each in half before serving.

FRIED ONION CAKES

IMPERIAL/METRIC	AMERICAN
1 lb./450 g. flour	4 cups flour
1 pint/6 dcl. water	2½ cups water
2 bunches spring onions	2 bunches scallions
6 tablespoons melted lard	½ cup melted lard
salt	salt

METHOD

Knead the flour and water together to make a soft dough. Divide into six and shape each piece into a round about 12 inches across.

Wash and finely chop the spring onions (scallions). Spread 1 tablespoon melted fat over each round and sprinkle ⅙ of the chopped spring onions (scallions) over. Sprinkle each with ½ teaspoon salt and roll up tightly like a pancake. Fold each in half and twist into an upstanding spiral. Flatten with a rolling pin and re-roll to a round about 6 inches across.

Fry each cake in shallow oil over medium heat for 2 minutes on each side. Reduce the heat to very low, cover the pan and cook each cake for another 3 minutes on each side. Cut each round into six wedges and serve piping hot.

SPRING ROLLS

IMPERIAL/METRIC	AMERICAN
$\frac{1}{2}$ lb./250 g. minced lean pork	$\frac{1}{2}$ lb. ground lean pork
4 oz./125 g. peeled shrimps	4 oz. peeled shrimps
1 tablespoon oil	1 tablespoon oil
2 spring onions	2 scallions
$\frac{1}{2}$ lb./250 g. bean sprouts	$\frac{1}{2}$ lb. bean sprouts
1 tablespoon soy sauce	1 tablespoon soy sauce
1 teaspoon salt	1 teaspoon salt
pinch of brown sugar	pinch of brown sugar
$\frac{1}{2}$ lb./225 g. flour	2 cups flour
1 pint/3 dcl. water	$2\frac{1}{2}$ cups water
1 egg	1 egg
deep fat for frying	deep fat for frying

METHOD

Mix the pork and shrimps together. Fry in oil for 2 minutes. Wash and finely chop the spring onions (scallions); drain the bean sprouts and add both to the pork. Mix well and cook for 2 minutes. Stir in the soy sauce, salt and sugar.

Mix the flour, water and egg to a smooth batter. Using a heavy-based frying pan (skillet), lightly greased, make 16 very thin pancakes, cooked on one side only. Place some of the mixture in the centre. Fold the edge nearest you to the centre, fold both sides in to the centre, then roll up, sealing last edge with a little water. Make all the rolls like this, then fry in hot, deep fat for about 15 minutes, turning the rolls during cooking to ensure even browning. Drain and serve.

Spring rolls

DESSERTS

The Chinese do not make a great production of the sweet course as we do in the West. A few sweet items may be included in the meal to add variety and to provide something to nibble between dishes, but they usually finish the meal with a fresh fruit like lychees. There are, however, a number of sweet dishes which make a pleasant ending to a Chinese meal.

JUJUBE CAKES

IMPERIAL/METRIC	AMERICAN
½ lb./250 g. jujubes (hung tsou) or dates	½ lb. jujubes (hung tsou) or dates
½ lb./250 g. glutinous rice flour	½ lb. glutinous rice flour

METHOD

Put the jujubes in a pan, cover with cold water and bring to the boil; simmer for 1 hour or until soft. Drain, then remove the skins and stones. If using dates, remove the stones and heat the dates slightly to soften the fruit. Beat the fruit to form a paste. Add the rice flour and knead together to make a soft dough.

Roll out to ¼ inch thick and cut out small shapes, using fancy cutters.

Steam the cakes in a steaming tier or on a greased, fine mesh rack over a pan of boiling water for 5 minutes.

NOTE: The cakes will remain soft if glutinous rice flour is used. If this is unobtainable, use ordinary rice flour, but do not be alarmed when the cakes harden after cooking.

GINGERED FRUIT

IMPERIAL/METRIC	AMERICAN
15 oz./450 g. canned pineapple pieces	15 oz. canned pineapple pieces
11 oz./330 g. canned lychees	11 oz. canned lychees
1 tablespoon chopped glacé cherries	1 tablespoon chopped glacé cherries
2 tablespoons chopped crystallized ginger	2 tablespoons chopped crystallized ginger
1 oz./30 g. flaked browned almonds	¼ cup flaked toasted almonds

METHOD

Drain the syrup from the canned fruits. Lightly combine the pineapple, lychees, glacé cherries and ginger in a serving bowl. Chill well. Sprinkle the almonds on top and serve immediately.

WHEAT CAKES

IMPERIAL/METRIC	AMERICAN
¾ lb./340 g. flour	3 cups flour
¾ pint/4 dcl. almost boiling water	1⅞ cups almost boiling water
3 tablespoons oil	¼ cup oil

METHOD

Knead the flour and water together to make a soft dough. Roll out very thinly and cut out 24 rounds, each 2 inches in diameter. Brush 12 of the rounds with oil and press the other 12 rounds on top. Roll each to a larger round about 6 inches across.

Using a heavy-based frying pan, lightly greased, fry each round over a low heat for 3 minutes on each side, under a tight fitting lid.

Pile the cooked wheat cakes, sometimes called doilies, on a plate and serve covered with a cloth. To eat the wheat cakes, separate each layer; this is easily done because of the oil used to sandwich them together.

Caramel apples

CARAMEL APPLES

IMPERIAL/METRIC	AMERICAN
6 apples	6 apples
1½ oz./45 g. plain flour	1½ oz. all-purpose flour
¼ oz./15 g. cornflour	¼ oz. cornstarch
2 egg whites	2 egg whites
oil for deep frying	oil for deep frying
4 oz./115 g. granulated sugar	½ cup granulated sugar
1 tablespoon oil	1 tablespoon oil
1 tablespoon sesame seeds	1 tablespoon sesame seeds

METHOD

Peel, core and quarter the apples. Dust them lightly with some of the plain (all-purpose) flour.

Sift remaining flour with cornflour (cornstarch) into a mixing bowl. Add egg whites and mix to a paste. Add the apple quarters and stir to coat with paste. Deep fry in hot oil until golden. Drain well. Place the sugar in a saucepan with 2 tablespoons water. Heat, stirring, until sugar has dissolved. Add the oil and continue heating slowly until sugar caramelises and is a light golden brown. Stir in the apple and sesame seeds. Serve immediately in lightly oiled dishes. Place a bowl of cold water on the table so that guests may drop the apple in the water to harden the caramel before eating.

MOW FLOWER TWISTS

IMPERIAL/METRIC	AMERICAN
½ lb./230 g. plain flour	2 cups all-purpose flour
4 oz./115 g. butter	½ cup butter
4 oz./115 g. granulated sugar	½ cup granulated sugar
1 oz./30 g. ground almonds	3 tablespoons ground almonds
1 egg	1 egg
½ teaspoon almond essence	½ teaspoon almond essence
oil for deep frying	oil for deep frying
icing sugar	icing sugar

METHOD

Sift the flour into a bowl and rub in the margarine or butter with the fingertips until the mixture resembles breadcrumbs. Stir in the sugar and ground almonds. Add the egg and essence and knead very well to make a pliable dough, adding a little water if necessary.

Roll the dough into a sausage about 1 inch in diameter and cut off 1 inch lengths. Roll each piece into a ribbon about 9–10 inches long, fold in half and twist twice. Take the ends of the ribbon back to the fold and push through the loop. Fry these twists in deep hot oil and cook until golden. Drain well; sprinkle with icing sugar and serve cold.

ALMOND CREAM WITH CHOW CHOW

IMPERIAL/METRIC	AMERICAN
1 lb./½ kg. canned chow chow or mixed fruit salad	1 lb. canned chow chow or mixed fruit salad
1 pint/6 dcl. water	2½ cups water
1 oz. gelatine	1 oz. unflavored gelatin
¾ pint/4 dcl. milk	2 cups milk
granulated sugar to taste	granulated sugar to taste
1 teaspoon almond essence	1 teaspoon almond essence

METHOD

Chop the larger pieces of chow chow in half or drain the mixed fruit salad.

Place 4 tablespoons of the water in a cup and stand it in a saucepan of hot water. Shower the gelatine into the cup and heat, stirring, until the gelatine has dissolved. Cool.

Heat the remaining water with milk, sugar to taste, and almond essence; stir until the sugar has dissolved. Stir in the gelatine. Pour into a shallow, lightly oiled cake tin and cool until set.

Cut the almond cream into triangular bite-sized pieces. Place these in a serving bowl with the fruit and combine very gently. Serve very cold.

NOTE: Chow Chow is Chinese preserved fruit which can be bought in shops specializing in Chinese groceries.

ALMOND LAKE WITH MANDARIN ORANGES

IMPERIAL/METRIC	AMERICAN
1 pint/6 dcl. milk	2½ cups milk
4 oz./125 g. granulated sugar	½ cup granulated sugar
1 teaspoon almond essence	1 teaspoon almond essence
2 oz./60 g. ground rice	⅓ cup ground rice
11 oz./325 g. canned mandarin oranges	11 oz. canned mandarin oranges
1 oz./30 g. flaked browned almonds	¼ cup flaked toasted almonds

METHOD

Put the milk, sugar, essence and rice in a saucepan. Bring to the boil, stirring constantly, and simmer for 5 minutes. Pour into a dish, cover and cool. Drain the mandarin oranges well. Spoon the rice into individual dishes. Place the mandarin oranges on the rice and sprinkle with the almonds.

*Almond lake
with mandarin oranges*

Almond cream with chow chow

FRIED SWEET POTATO

IMPERIAL/METRIC
1 lb./½ kg. sweet potatoes
shallow oil for frying
6 tablespoons syrup

AMERICAN
1 lb. sweet potatoes
shallow oil for frying
⅓ cup syrup

METHOD
Thickly peel the potato and cut into sticks about ½ inch wide and 2–3 inches long – similar to chips. Dry the sticks on a clean towel and fry them in the oil for about 4 minutes or until golden brown and crisp. Drain and pile on a large dish. Heat the syrup and pour over the chips: serve.
NOTE: If obtainable, use the small sweet potatoes as they are easier to handle.

EIGHT TREASURES RICE

IMPERIAL/METRIC	AMERICAN	METHOD
6 oz./180 g. short grain rice	¾ cup short grain rice	Cook the rice in boiling water for about 15 minutes or until tender. Drain and stir in the sugar.
4 oz./125 g. brown sugar	⅔ cup brown sugar	
2 oz./60 g. dates	½ cup dates	Place a layer of rice in the base of an oiled 1½–2 pint pudding bowl. Add a layer of fruit and nuts to make a pattern, pressing it through the rice so that it will be seen as decoration when the pudding is unmoulded. Add another layer of rice, then a layer of mixed nuts and fruit. Continue layering until all the ingredients have been used, finishing with a layer of rice.
2 oz./60 g. blanched almonds	½ cup blanched almonds	
2 oz./60 g. walnuts	½ cup walnuts	
2 oz./60 g. glacé cherries	⅓ cup glacé cherries	
2 oz./60 g. mixed peel	½ cup mixed peel	Press down very firmly and cover with greased greaseproof (waxed) paper or aluminium foil. Place the bowl in a steamer over gently boiling water, or in a saucepan with simmering water coming halfway up the side of the bowl. Cook for 30–40 minutes. Unmould and serve hot.
2 oz./60 g. raisins	¼ cup raisins	
2 oz./60 g. glacé pineapple, apricots, or figs as available	⅓ cup glacé pineapple, apricots, or figs as available	

ALMOND TEA JELLY

IMPERIAL/METRIC	AMERICAN	METHOD
4 oz./115 g. ground almonds	½ cup ground almonds	Mix the almonds and rice in a bowl with 2 pints (1⅓ litre/5 cups) cold water, cover and leave for 2 hours. Strain through fine muslin into a large bowl. Add the milk and mix well.
2 tablespoons ground rice	2 tablespoons ground rice	
½ pint/3 dcl. milk	1¼ cups milk	
2 tablespoons sugar	2 tablespoons sugar	Stand the bowl in a large saucepan with enough boiling water to come halfway up the sides of the bowl. Cover and simmer for 2 hours, stirring occasionally.
1 teaspoon gelatine	1 teaspoon unflavored gelatin	

Add the sugar, stir well and leave to cool slightly. Mix the gelatine with 2 tablespoons hot water until dissolved. Stir into the milk mixture when almost cold. Mix well and pour into a shallow serving dish. Leave until set.

ALMOND BISCUITS

IMPERIAL/METRIC	AMERICAN	METHOD
¾ lb./340 g. plain flour	3 cups all-purpose flour	Sift the flour, baking powder and salt into a bowl. Cream the margarine (or butter) and sugar together until light, white and fluffy. Beat in the egg and almond essence. Stir in the sifted dry ingredients to make a stiff dough.
2 teaspoons baking powder	2 teaspoons baking powder	
4 oz./115 g. margarine or butter	½ cup margarine or butter	
½ lb./230 g. granulated sugar	1 cup granulated sugar	Form the mixture into balls about 1–1½ inch diameter and place these on a greased baking tray. Place half an almond (split lengthways) on each ball and press to flatten slightly. Brush with beaten egg.
1 egg	1 egg	
1 teaspoon almond essence	1 teaspoon almond essence	
blanched almonds for decoration	blanched almonds for decoration	Bake in a moderate oven (350°F/180°C, Mark 4) for 20 minutes or until golden. Cool on a wire rack. This quantity makes about 45 biscuits.
beaten egg for glazing	beaten egg for glazing	

Eight treasures rice

SPECIAL DISHES

Although all the recipes in this book are suitable for serving as part of a Chinese feast, which may include up to 30 dishes, there are some special dishes which are particularly suitable for entertaining and which need less preparation than a large number of courses. The nearest equivalents in the West to these dishes are the barbecue and the fondue, which provide an informal meal which the hostess can enjoy as much as the guests.

FIREPOT

IMPERIAL/METRIC	AMERICAN
1 chicken	1 chicken
2 lb./1 kg. pork or lamb tenderloin	2 lb. pork or lamb tenderloin
2 lb./1 kg. sole or plaice	2 lb. sole or flounder
¾ lb./375 g. lamb's liver	¾ lb. lamb's liver
½ lb./250 g. pea starch noodles	½ lb. pea starch noodles
1 bunch spring onions	1 bunch scallions
2 pints/1 litre chicken stock	5 cups chicken stock
6 tablespoons soy sauce	½ cup soy sauce
3 cloves garlic	3 cloves garlic
1 tablespoon chopped fresh ginger	1 tablespoon chopped fresh ginger
2 teaspoons chilli sauce	2 teaspoons chili sauce
6 tablespoons fermented soya bean paste	½ cup fermented soya bean paste
6 tablespoons oil	½ cup oil

METHOD

Bone the chicken and cut all the meat into very fine Chinese slices. Arrange on several plates. Skin the fish and cut the flesh into paper-thin slices. Wash the liver, remove the membranes and cut the flesh into paper-thin slices. Soak the noodles in hot water for at least 30 minutes before serving. Trim the onions (scallions) and cut into short lengths. Heat the stock to boiling just before serving. Arrange all the ingredients separately on several plates.

Put the soy sauce, crushed garlic, chopped ginger, chilli sauce, paste and oil into a large screw-top jar and shake vigorously until all the ingredients are evenly blended. Divide evenly between the guests' individual bowls.

The next step is purely guest participation. The Chinese use a special pot called a boiling fire pot which is a large brass bowl, the centre of which is shaped into a tall funnel. The funnel is filled with charcoal and the surrounding pot then filled with boiling stock and placed in the centre of the table with all the raw, prepared ingredients surrounding it. It is very difficult to get these pots in the West, but a large shallow casserole dish placed on a table spirit burner makes an ideal substitute, with another spirit burner keeping the extra stock hot until it is needed to replenish the cooking pot.

To eat this great assortment of goodies, one takes a pair of chopsticks or a spoon and fork and selects an item of food, dips it momentarily in the boiling stock, then transfers it to one's own sauce bowl before eating.

Firepot

VELVETEEN OF PORK

IMPERIAL/METRIC	AMERICAN
2 lb./1 kg. pork tenderloin	2 lb. pork tenderloin
½ pint/¼ litre chicken stock	1¼ cups chicken stock
2 tablespoons peanut oil	2 tablespoons peanut oil
3 tablespoons soy sauce	¼ cup soy sauce
2 tablespoons sherry	2 tablespoons sherry
pinch of brown sugar	pinch of brown sugar
pinch of salt	pinch of salt
½ teaspoon fermented soya bean paste	½ teaspoon fermented soya bean paste

METHOD

Cut the meat into ½ inch cubes, put them in a pan with the chicken stock, bring to the boil, cover and simmer very gently for about 2 hours, or until the pork is falling apart. Drain off any remaining stock.

Heat the oil in a deep saucepan, add the pork and fry over a fierce heat, stirring all the time for 4–5 minutes. Add the soy sauce, sherry, sugar, salt and soya bean paste. Mix well and continue to fry the mixture over a very low heat for about 10 minutes, stirring all the time, until the ingredients blend together to form a thick, paste-like substance.

Serve cold on snippets of toasted or fried bread as appetizers.

NOTE: The velveteen can be stored in a screw-top jar and a teaspoonful added to vegetable dishes for flavour, rather like our own potted meats which, although cooked slightly differently, produce a softened, cooked meat paste.

BRAZIER LAMB

IMPERIAL/METRIC	AMERICAN
1 large leg of lamb, or 1 tenderloin per person	1 large leg of lamb, or 1 tenderloin per person
1 egg per person	1 egg per person
4 cloves garlic	4 cloves garlic
5 spring onions	5 scallions
4 tablespoons soy sauce	⅓ cup soy sauce
4 tablespoons fermented soya bean paste	⅓ cup fermented soya bean paste
4 tablespoons sweet soya bean jam or redcurrant jelly, dissolved	⅓ cup sweet soya bean jam or redcurrant jelly, dissolved
2 teaspoons chilli sauce	2 tablespoons chili sauce
4 tablespoons oil	⅓ cup oil

METHOD

Cut the meat into very fine slices and divide evenly between each guest's plate. Break one egg into each bowl. Crush the garlic and put into a large screw top jar. Chop the onions (scallions) very finely and add with the remaining ingredients to the garlic. Secure the lid and shake vigorously to blend the ingredients evenly. Divide this into further small bowls, one per person.

At this stage the guests take over. A charcoal fire, which has been burning until glowing stage is reached, is placed on the table and covered with a fine mesh rack to prevent the pieces of meat from falling into the embers.

Next, each guest is served one or two plates of meat, one bowl containing the egg and another bowl containing sauce. The idea is to use very long chopsticks (fondue forks make an ideal tool for the uninitiated), and to pick up a piece of meat, hold it over the fire for a few seconds (no more, as the intense heat soon cooks the fine slices), and dip it first in the raw egg, then in the sauce, before eating.

Like outdoor barbecues, this is an informal yet exciting method of eating and one which is guaranteed to break the ice in situations where most of the guests do not know each other. The meal does tend to go on, though, as the fascination of doing one's own cooking at someone else's table seems to increase the appetite, and it is sometimes difficult to keep track of how much one has actually consumed.

Acknowledgements

American Rice Council: P53
Brown & Polson: P69
Canned & Packaged Food Bureau: P75
The Fruit Producers' Council: P26, 117
Syndication International: P14, 27, 71
John West: P49, 118
Young's Seafoods: P80